The Gospel According to Facebook:

Social Media and the Good News

Rev. Bruce H. Joffe, Ph.D.

"The Gospel According to Facebook: Social Media and the Good News," by Bruce H. Joffe. ISBN 978-1-62137-448-0 (softcover); ISBN 978-1-62137-449-7 (eBook).

Library of Congress Number: 2014901170

Published 2014 by Virtualbookworm.com Publishing Inc, P.O. Box 9949, College Station, TX 77842, US. ©2014, Bruce H. Joffe. All rights reserved. No part of this publication may be reproduced, stored in a retrieval system, or transmitted in any form or by any means, electronic, mechanical, recording or otherwise, without the prior written permission of Bruce H. Joffe.

Manufactured in the United States of America.

The Gospel According to Facebook:

Social Media and the Good News

Rev. Bruce H. Joffe, Ph.D.

Also by Bruce H. Joffe:

The Scapegoat

A Hint of Homosexuality?
'Gay' and Homoerotic Imagery in American Print Advertising

Square Peg in a Round Hole

Personal PR:
Public Relations and Marketing Tips
That Work to Your Advantage

Contents

Author's Apologetics 1

PART ONE

The Gospel According to Facebook: A New Testament

The Gospel: According to …? 11
Importance of the Message 14
What Will You Wear to the Wedding? 23
A Bigger and Better God 30
Elizabeth's Story: Amazing Grace! 38
Eunuchs and Gender Identity 43
Social Justice and the Kingdom of God 49
The Heart of the Matter 59
Christian Branding 81
When Old Wine Skins No Longer Fit 93
Doing Church Differently 105

PART TWO

Social Media and the Good News

Preface 121
Collected Wisdom and Proverbs 131

The Gospel ...
According to
Facebook

AUTHOR'S APOLOGETICS

I've been a Facebook fan and follower for some time now.

Fearsome to some and fulfilling for others, I have found this magical, mystical *tour de force* of technology to be a phenomenon that has impacted me both personally and professionally. It has reunited and put me in touch with many people I've known along the trajectory of my life, just as, exponentially, it has connected me to other people I've come to know online and now consider my "friends."

Similarly, this social networking service has helped me find comfort, succor, support, and suggestions from an extension of others involved with spiritual matters who are also engaged in prayer, theological discourse, and practical concerns of church polity and governance.

As a pastor, I find myself tending a vital yet amorphous congregation with the same cares and concerns shared by my "real" one. We talk about our convictions, pray, share, enjoy spiritual music, create events, and come together much like other churches do. And, absurd as it may seem, we grow by word-of-mouth testimony as one Facebook user recommends (or *Likes*) us enough to link our beliefs with another … and another … and yet another.

We've assembled what, to all intents and purposes, is a congregation.

And, ironically, it's an evangelical one at that.

Since I am virtually connected to an increasing number of people who think like I do in terms of the Christian faith, daily I am able to see, read, respond to, and share what they're opining and expressing so openly online.

Increasingly, I find myself responding with "Likes" and "Comments" to a host of images (sometimes accompanied by commentary) that people post on Facebook. So, I created a separate folder in my computer's picture collection for those graphics that struck a spiritual chord within me.

I first used a number of these visions and views by editing and organizing them into a PowerPoint presentation for guiding principles and anecdotal purposes in a community-based seminar entitled, "Who Speaks for God?"

Here's what the printed catalog said about my cursillo:

Did the Divine actually speak to us ... maybe, even, using Democratic or Republican rhetoric? Why is the vocabulary of some theologies peaceful and gracious, while others tend to be threatening and damning? What place do holy books have in editorializing the language and lexicon of who and what we worship? Is there gender within (and without) spiritual speech? Did the supernatural tell us that we must be "exclusionary," keeping all but the holiest out ... or "inclusionary," finding a place at the table for all?

Yet, perhaps, the Creative Force – the One we will refer to as "God" – hasn't stopped talking, but is still speaking and trying to tell us something (even) today? What might that be?

Whether focused on the hereafter or more concerned, instead, with today and tomorrow ... regardless of one's theology and belief system ... there is much to be learned from the world's great religions about the things "most surely believed among us" (Luke 1:1) as well as the peculiar practices or beliefs that tend to divide us.

Mary Baldwin College Professor Bruce H. Joffe, Ph.D., an ordained pastor, will lead this two-session interactive discussion about the myriad voices clamoring to be heard today—all in the name of God.

As my collection of Facebook posts concerning religion and spirituality continued to grow, I began to think about compiling a series of these comments that reflected people's attitudes about their faith and beliefs – especially Christianity – into a book of meditations.

And once I started to sort and organize this collection of vignettes into a narrative of certain coherence, I came to realize that I needed an appropriate context – hermeneutics, if you will – for transposing the Gospel message from its traditional highways and byways onto a new and different delivery method or medium: the Internet. More specifically, the social networks available via the World Wide Web. And even more precisely, Facebook.

"With more than 500 million users, Facebook has become the dominant player in the social networking industry," claims hubspot.com, a marketing-oriented website.

That was back in June 2010. By September 2011, Facebook had "reached over 750 million users in the world," according to the online encyclopedia, Wikipedia. In September 2013, Facebook reported passing 1.19 billion monthly active users, 874 million mobile users, and 728 million daily users.

Facebook's marketing mantra speaks to its efficacy in "customer acquisition," whether those customers are businesses, consumers, or churches and church-goers. "67% of B2C (business-to-consumer) companies and 41% of B2B (business-to-business) companies have acquired a customer from Facebook. With over 955 million people on Facebook, there are probably some customers waiting for you on there, too," marvels a free eBook entitled *How to Attract Customers with Facebook*.

Facebook informs, promotes comments, connects, corrects, and provides a public pulpit for sharing ... much like a town meeting with feedback.

When it comes to faith and proclaiming one's religious beliefs, however, transitioning from the contemplative to the illustrative becomes a challenge.

Back in 2008, Luke Miedema wrote in his *Every Square Inch* blog: "Facebook was established with the assumption that we live in community and its goal, its gospel, is to enhance the level of that community by bringing it into a new sphere with new possibilities: the web."

Miedema maintains that the Gospel according to Facebook is that we need to promote community: "Actually, now that we speak about it in those terms, (this) doesn't sound too dissimilar from God's statement in Genesis 2:18, that 'It is not good for man to be alone.'"

From the very beginning, he said, the Bible "makes it abundantly clear that we were intended to live in community with other people. God is a community within himself and, being made in His image, we carry the same innate need for intimate connections with other people. Many passages in the New Testament, in fact, are devoted to developing and enhancing the quality of our human community."

He concluded that Facebook and the Bible share the same fundamental assumption: we must promote human community.

One question is whether Facebook promotes a biblical version of community. Does it help us live more in line with the Bible's vision for human interaction? Is it a help or a hindrance? Does the Facebook community, perhaps, promote a more Christian message than our churches and religious establishment ... or does it serve to make a mockery of what, traditionally, has been sacrosanct?

To answer that, it would be helpful to understand how the Bible depicts a spiritual community. More important to the Christian, however, is discerning the message of Jesus about how we are to live in a Kingdom of God here and now. Remember how he responded when asked how we are to pray?

"Your kingdom come, your will be done ... on earth as it is in heaven."

Jesus says the greatest commandment is to love God with all our heart, strength, soul, and mind ... and that the second is like it: to love others as we would love ourselves (Matthew 22:38, 39).

Christ calls us to an other-oriented view of relationships, to be concerned about the best for another person, just as we normally would for ourselves.

Because of the Internet and its social media connections, the entrenched forces of organized religion everywhere are now being challenged by a dynamic new testament. Voices previously unheard now trumpet their messages across time and space, reaching and rallying an audience that's receptive and responsive.

The good news shared by the social media echoes the message of Jesus about grace, love, peace, compassion, inclusion, and social justice for all.

That's the Gospel according to Facebook.

No longer is it possible for the church to conduct its "business as usual."

Facebook won't allow good deeds and bad, blessings and curses, to go unnoticed; no, it rewards the messages it likes and chastises those it doesn't.

As I began thinking about possible relationships between Facebook and the Gospel, I remembered John Berendt's book, *Midnight in the Garden of Good and Evil*, published in 1994.

The gothic spellbinder about Savannah begins with an account describing people, places, and personalities of this eccentric Southern town, providing context and positioning us for what is to come in the second part…when the plot moves on to tell the story of supposedly real-life events occurring in the 1980s when a local male hustler allegedly is murdered by an iconic yet well respected antiques dealer.

My book bears no resemblance to Berendt's bestseller, except for the sharp contrast between each book's two parts.

But both parts <u>are</u> connected.

Clearly, the same must be said of the Bible with its Old and New Testaments (or Covenants): Hebrew and Christian.

Like the Bible and even *Midnight in the Garden of Good and Evil,* my *Gospel According to Facebook* is about the effects of principled communication on an engaged – and, at times, enraged – and interconnected community.

"Sacred cows make the best hamburger."

–Mark Twain

Part One

A New Testament

THE GOSPEL: ACCORDING TO …?

Whither the Gospel?

That depends upon whom you ask:

To evangelical and fundamentalist Christians, it usually becomes a matter of salvation, as in John 3:16. "For God so loved the world that he gave his one and only Son, that whoever believes in him shall not perish but have eternal life."

To other, more mainstream Christians, it often refers to a revised and updated understanding – a new covenant – with God: of God's relationship to us and ours with God.

To Jews around the time of Jesus, it was expected to be about liberation from bondage and freedom from their oppressors brought about by the person of a prophesied Messiah in their Hebrew Scriptures; while to some more contemporary Jews and others victimized by a belligerent Christianity of pious pogroms, exclusion, expulsion, extreme extermination, and holy crusades, it has meant malice, hatred, and death by denial.

To African-American slaves and all those forced into servitude even today, it is about hope: faith and belief in a better world than this yet to come.

To some, it's about forgiveness … to others, it's a new understanding of behavioral standards and expectations … and to yet others, it's a lovely holiday story.

And to those who were there, for those who had witnessed the wretched crucifixion and remarkable resurrection of Jesus, it was good news indeed worth sharing: "The Lord is risen!" his beloved followers shouted, sharing their message from place to place.

The Gospel was probably quite different before, during, and after the life of Jesus. Depending upon who you were – a Jew praying for God's deliverance and freedom from bondage through a mighty Messiah ... a "gentile" worshipping myriad gods of the natural and supernatural worlds ... a person who actually had heard Jesus teach and preach, reforming his or her own understanding of what the hitherto holy writ in the Hebrew Testament truly meant ... or someone who was touched and healed by the mystery of faith in God and God's messenger – your understanding of the Gospel was transfixed.

For those living and experiencing Jesus while he walked among them, some (maybe even most) still didn't "get it"; despite his faithful rhetoric and "miraculous" demonstrations, even Jesus showed frustration at the lack of understanding expressed by his disciples (i.e., Matthew 16:21-23; Mark 6:52, 8:21, etc.).

Later, of course, those disciples-turned-apostles would demonstrate remarkable testimonies and deeds in the name of Jesus, the man they now acknowledged as the Christ.

A word of Anglo-Saxon origin, *Gospel* is the rendering of the Greek word "evangelion," or good message. According to the online dictionary.com, Gospel is a noun that refers to:

(1) the teachings of Jesus and the apostles; the Christian revelation.

(2) the story of Christ's life and teachings, especially as contained in the first four books of the new testament, namely Matthew, Mark, Luke, and John.

(3) any of these four books.

(4) something regarded as true and implicitly believed.

(5) a doctrine regarded as of prime importance.

(6) glad tidings, especially concerning salvation and the kingdom of God as announced to the world by Christ.

(7) ecclesiastical, an extract from one of the four Gospels, forming part of the Eucharistic service.

(8) gospel music.

In addition, as an adjective, Gospel is said to mean:

(9) of, pertaining to, or proclaiming the gospel or its teachings.

(10) in accordance with the gospel; evangelical.

(11) of or pertaining to gospel music.

Yet, lost or forgotten in whatever meaning may be given to the Gospel is that it definitely is a <u>message</u>: a message to be shared.

Sharing messages is one of the indulgences that Facebook likes best.

IMPORTANCE OF THE MESSAGE

Language scholars and linguists, professors and theorists, agree that a "message" is essential and integral to all communication. But while some go on to define communication as an "exchange of information," others prefer dubbing it the "exchange of meaning."

The differences are profound.

Take the narratives about Jesus of Nazareth, for example.

Exchanging information would be a message that a Jewish man named Jesus, apparently innocent of wrong-doing, was crucified and killed by Pontius Pilate's decree. Three days later, believe it or not, he was found to yet live.

Exchanging meaning, however, would take this information and place it into a context that, based on an understanding of the Hebrew Scriptures, the man named Jesus of Nazareth fulfilled all what was foretold of Israel's Messiah. Despite the fact that the rabbis – teachers – didn't grasp it … or did but feared the consequences of what interpreting the Bible this way might mean to the future of their people (and themselves), Jesus indeed was and is the Messiah.

That's why the different constructs used to introduce this chapter are so critically important. Depending on who and what you are, where and when you live, your interpretation and understanding of this man named Jesus and his message are skewed.

For some it means one thing; for others, something else.

Undoubtedly, the Gospel is quite different to the Christian, the Jew, and the Muslim. It's different to the Catholic and the Protestant. Its meanings may even abide in subtle yet profound differences between Baptists, Episcopalians, Lutherans, Presbyterians, Methodists, Mormons, and Seventh Day Adventists.

Scripture always has been a matter of translation, interpretation, and context. But by <u>whom</u> and according to <u>whose</u> traditions? Responsible, faithful people who carefully study the words contained in the canon can – and will – often reach different conclusions.

The Message in Communication

Why do such differences occur? What brought them about? Whose sense of truth trumps another's? Where and when do we know what to believe?

Ultimately, I suspect, it comes down to how we communicate.

In its most basic form, communication involves three basic elements:

     (1)   A source from which the communication originates;
     (2)   A message that the source sends; and
     (3)   A recipient to whom that message is directed.

For simplicity's sake, let's say that, in terms of the Gospel, the source is God. The Creator. Ultimate Being. Sacred Essence. Or whatever name(s) you feel comfortable using when referring to this absolute, infinite entity. Similarly, we'll propose that the recipient to whom God is directing the message is us: humanity, "mankind," creation.

Okay? Fair enough so far …

... except that when it comes to defining what we mean by the "message," we are entangled in a web of possibilities proposed by communication experts.

Here's why:

Some will argue that the message is simply its content: what it says. Period. You've probably heard it said what some Christians believe about the Bible: "God said it. I believe it. That's all there is to it." For them, the content of the Bible is inerrant. Its truth in everything it says is above and without question.

Personally, I believe the Bible is our story about how we've evolved from Creation to creating specific societies and civilizations—in particular, the Israelites in the Old Testament and the Christian in the New.

While there may have been reasons – at a given time and/or place – that the Bible banned certain practices, Christians should approach all Scripture through the prism of Christ Jesus: What did Jesus say about something? To whom? When and why? And what didn't he say? Why not?

What really matters here and what doesn't?

The "Word of God," as interpreted by anyone other than Jesus, must never be allowed to become what Adrian Thatcher condemns in *The Savage Text: The Use and Abuse of the Bible* as an inhumane handbook that justifies preferred prejudices or brutalizes behavior.

The Christian who believes homosexuality to be an abominable sin against God, for example, invariably points to the Bible as justification for this belief. What else can he or she do? Such a person isn't about to blame himself for his bigotry. No other "proof" exists that gay people offend God. Challenge some Christians to make a single argument for homosexuality being wrong that doesn't quote or reference the Bible and suddenly they're in a house of mirrors, pointing to themselves. So they convince themselves that, "Yes, it <u>does</u> say so in the Bible! The Bible <u>does</u> condemn homosexuality!"

For those who believe the Bible contains a specific answer to any given question, the book must be studied, memorized verbatim, to capture every word, nuance, all the laws, precept, jot and tittle necessary to understand all those sometimes confusing and – I daresay – ambiguous rules and regulations contained in that collection of "God stories" denoted in the Bible.

Trouble is, which Bible? And in what language? Hebrew, Greek, Aramaic, or English? The King James Version? The New King James Version? The Revised Standard Version? The New International Version? The Living Bible? The Message Bible in Contemporary Language by Eugene Peterson?

The Medium Is the Message

You think that's not important? Think again.

Philosopher and communication theorist H. Marshall McLuhan introduced a media theory with many practical applications. Best known as "the medium is the message," McLuhan proposed that the true meaning of a message is better determined not by its content, per se, but by its delivery mechanism.

For instance, a newscast story about a heinous crime may be less about the "news" itself — the content — and more about public attitudes towards, say, gun control that the newscast engenders by bringing such horrible crimes into our homes to watch over dinner, while relaxing in the living room, or getting ready for bed. Similarly, the constant stream of negative political rhetoric broadcast continuously during election campaigns causes us to become bitter about candidates, their ideals, and even our neighbors who support them.

Depending upon our perspective, we interpret news and/or commentary carried by Fox News differently than the content brought to us by CNN or CNBC. Or we're more likely to believe what we read in the *New York Times* than the *New York Daily News*. Or, for that matter, what we're told in one person's blog vs. another's. According to how we perceive the medium, we will accept, deny, or otherwise judge the veracity and value of its content.

The same can be said of churches, contextually.

What we believe about the Divine is a function of the religious environment in which it is presented. Depending upon the denomination or church tradition, we derive our perspective(s) on how to define and approach what's holy. Through pomp and circumstance? Rote and ritual? Speaking in tongues or singing in the spirit? Silence and solitude? Following a specific liturgy, liturgical calendar, and lectionary? Or going with the flow and rolling with the pastor's pundits and punches?

What that message is about really does make a difference.

The Gospel message actually has been broadcast by churches and their respective media: books, magazines, radio, television ... and, now, online. Which is why – some people will tell you – we tend to fellowship around our differences instead of those things we surely believe in common.

Because the medium, in fact, can actually be the message – especially among the social media – the content of a Facebook Gospel can and will differ, depending upon who sends and receives it.

Since only what's posted by my Facebook "friends" and *likers* (who, by and large, share the same values and beliefs as I do) tends to be seen by me, my Facebook messages will differ from those of others—including yours.

Therefore it follows that those aligned online with Christians more progressive in their theology will receive messages whose senders (sources) and apologetics (content) arguably are radically and diametrically different from Facebook messages sent and seen by/from those more "fundamentally" oriented and aligned.

This, then, is a critical difference in sharing the Gospel message as a function of the social media: By its populist nature and design, more people have input to disseminating information and opinions, as well as to build on them through online contributions which can support, reinforce, refine and/or refute the message about God that someone originally posted. How very different a world from that where bombast from the bully pulpit determines acceptable messages and a preacher's messages are unilaterally oriented.

Maybe, 'Who' Matters More than 'What' in a Message

Even so, whether it's the content or the medium that determines the true meaning of a message is rivaled by yet a third arbiter: According to this rule, the messenger – i.e., the person – can be so commanding as to engulf and dwarf any other interpretation. That is, the person or character is so captivating and "charismatic" that he (or she) transcends the medium and the content to, substantially, become the message in and of himself/herself.

John F. Kennedy. Adolf Hitler. Eleanor Roosevelt. Ronald Reagan. Princess Diana. Mother Teresa. Jim Jones. Martin Luther. Martin Luther King, Jr. Bill Clinton. Gandhi. Oprah Winfrey. Moses. John the Baptist. The Apostle Paul. The Dalai Lama. Nelson Mandela. Billy Graham. Walter Cronkite. Abraham Lincoln. Eva Perón. Mary Magdalene. Madonna.

Even Lady Gaga and the Kardashians, some might say.

People such as these affect and influence others at a deep emotional level, communicate effectively with them, and tend to make strong interpersonal connections. Whether we like them or not, we cannot help but respond to an unmistakable charm, "karma," or attraction inherent to each of these people. Their compelling nature apparently is more important than both the content and the medium of their message. In effect, they *are* the message.

Obviously, this can be said of Christ Jesus. As the Logos, he is the content, the real meaning, the Word incarnate of God. How many times did Jesus say (or imply), "You have heard it said… but I say unto you"?

The people marveled at what Jesus said because he said it with real meaning, not as their teachers of the Law had done when they argued and quibbled about scriptures over and again; no, here was one who spoke with authority, who unquestionably understood and told them what the words meant.

Message Conflicts as Content, Medium, and/or Person

Pope Francis is an excellent example of an enigma and the dichotomy of a message at odds with itself: When his message is taken personally, many adore the man as a good Christian; when it's taken as content, however, people may abhor the orthodox catechism he continues to profess.

"Within ten minutes of announcing that Pope Francis had been named *Time*'s 2013 Person of the Year, the news had been retweeted over 7,000 times and, within an hour, it had become a topic of discussion in some 130 countries," the magazine reported seven days later.

Opined Paul Feiner of Greenburgh, NY: "One doesn't have to be Jewish to love rye bread. And one doesn't have to be Catholic to appreciate the new Pope. He inspires people of all religions to care about others and to be better human beings."

"He is lighting the way for all of us," Maria Shriver said on Twitter.

But "why is he so dazzling?" asked Petula Dvorak at the *Washington Post*. "Because we live in a culture that has largely accepted greed and bad behavior as the norm."

The Vatican replied: "The Holy Father is not looking to become famous or to receive honors, but if the choice of Person of the Year helps spread the message of the Gospel – a message of God's love for everyone – he will certainly be happy about that."

Energizing communication in today's interconnected global community is a muse personified by the man, the message, and the media.

Perhaps the same should be inferred and implied about Jesus.

The Gospel of John aptly sums up the triune nature of a message's meaning – the content, the medium, the person – in the simple eloquence of its signature opening verse:

"In the beginning was the Word, and the Word was with God, and the Word was God." (John 1:1; KJV, NIV, RSV)

Here, we have <u>content</u> that provides three interrelated pieces of information: (1) Something called the "Word" existed in the very beginning; (2) This Word was with – or conjoined to – God; and (3) the Word itself actually was God.

Regardless of the <u>medium</u> – the King James, New International, or Revised Standard version of the Bible – the information presented here is the same. Yet only by presupposing that a person, Jesus, and this "Word" are synonymous does the text gain clarity in pretext, context, and meaning.

To truly understand John's intended message in this verse, we must interpret it as being about a specific <u>person</u>: Jesus. Thus we are told that, before anything came to be created or happened, something called the "Word" – located with God and then identified, in fact, as God – already existed. And, as the medium through which all things are made, Jesus is further defined by John (1:2-3) as both the incarnate Logos … and divine.

"He that hath ears to hear, let him hear," says the King James version in Matthew 11:15, while the Living Bible gives this translation of the same verse: "If ever you were willing to listen, listen now!"

Similarly, these two translations express the same sentiments of Jesus found in Mark 4:9 quite differently: "He that hath ears to hear, hear!" warns the King James. "If you have ears, listen!" urges the Living Bible.

Much ado about nothing, you wonder?

We shall soon see.

WHAT WILL YOU WEAR TO THE WEDDING?

The parable of the wedding banquet (or wedding feast, garment, guests) told in Matthew 22:1-14 is a good example of how the message can, at once, be understood in terms of its content, its medium, and/or its person(s). Depending on one's vantage point, the perspective – and message – will differ.

Here's how the parable appears in the Bible's New International version:

> Jesus spoke to them again in parables, saying: "The kingdom of heaven is like a king who prepared a wedding banquet for his son. He sent his servants to those who had been invited to the banquet to tell them to come, but they refused to come. Then he sent some more servants and said, 'Tell those who have been invited that I have prepared my dinner: My oxen and fattened cattle have been butchered, and everything is ready. Come to the wedding banquet.' But they paid no attention and went off—one to his field, another to his business. The rest of them seized his servants, mistreated them and killed them. The king was enraged. He sent his army and destroyed those murderers and burned their city. Then he said to his servants, 'The wedding banquet is ready, but those I invited did not deserve to

come. Go to the street corners and invite to the banquet anyone you find.' So the servants went out into the streets and gathered all the people they could find, both good and bad, and the wedding hall was filled with guests. But when the king came in to see the guests, he noticed a man there who was not wearing wedding clothes. 'Friend,' he asked, 'how did you get in here without wedding clothes?' The man was speechless. Then the king told the attendants, 'Tie him hand and foot, and throw him outside, into the darkness, where there will be weeping and gnashing of teeth.' For many are invited, but few are chosen.'"

Now, let's look at this passage in terms of divining its message:

Is the message its <u>content</u>?

The <u>medium</u> – i.e., manner or means – by which it is told?

Or the <u>persons</u> involved in it?

The wedding parable is the third of three, end-time parables about worthiness that Matthew has Jesus telling when he enters the Temple in Jerusalem at the Passover time and his authority is questioned. In the first, Jesus talks about a man who had two sons—one who said he would work in the vineyard, but didn't; the other said he wouldn't, but did.

The second is the parable of the talents, in which the Kingdom of God is taken away from renters who were supposed to sow and reap its vineyard to yield a harvest. When they didn't, the landowner rented his vineyard to others, who produced fruit.

Now we are told of the king planning a wedding banquet for his son to which many people have been invited but refuse to come. Then, he sweetens the invitation by describing the scrumptious food he's planning to serve. But still they won't come. So, instead, the king invites everyone – good people and bad, we're told – to the banquet. People come from near and far and enjoy the feast; but one person who's there, apparently, isn't dressed appropriately. The king asks him why his appearance doesn't show the proper respect due, under the circumstances, but the man has no reply. So, he's thrown outside and banished from the kingdom.

(A similar parable is told by Luke; but we must remember that this particular story appears in Matthew ... who was writing to Jewish people in an effort to introduce them to their Messiah and get them to believe that Jesus actually is the Christ.)

In that context, the beginning of the parable contains a message that makes sense to us: God had called a special people to be a nation of priests, testifying as witnesses to the one and only God ... encouraging others to follow their monotheism, mindful of the way.

But, despite the cries of prophets, time and again the people's focus shifted from the Holy One of Israel to their own self-centered desires and idols.

Then, one day, Almighty God became one with them ... yet, still they rejected him and refused to heed God's voice. So, ultimately, the very stone that the builders rejected became the cornerstone and foundation of faith for others.

Are you with me thus far?

Understanding the meaning and intent of this parable – this message – up to here isn't all that difficult. It becomes more challenging, however, when we get to the part about the wedding garment ... and it gets even more confusing with its footnote about many being called but few chosen.

Passages like these almost make me wish I had a more fundamentalist perspective, because it would make the meaning of this parable so much easier for me to translate.

According to fundamentalist Christology, the message here is found in the person of Jesus whose blood sacrifice for a world of sinners must be accepted (or not) in order for us to be "saved" … or cast aside, into "hell."

But I'm meandering.

Let's get back to the message – content, medium, or person? – of the wedding garment parable.

The guest invited to the king's wedding banquet knows what he's expected to wear, but deliberately chooses not to. In effect, he's looking at the king and spitting in his eye or slapping his face. "Yes, I'm here enjoying your food and the festivities," his attitude seems to be saying. "But I'll be damned if I change clothes or what I'm now wearing! I'm here on my terms, not yours."

To me, this invited guest who's been affirmed, included, and welcomed with love and compassion by his host, has committed that "unpardonable sin" by blaspheming the Holy Spirit.

Which is why he's been thrown out and no longer lives in God's Kingdom.

Whether or not he had a wedding garment to wear really is beside the point. Some theologians will say that kings often provided their guests with wedding garments, while other scholars will tell you that the king only required those invited to come in clean, not dirty, clothes.

Cleanliness, at least, is a badge of honor and respect if not a Christ-covered life of spotless spiritual character.

You may ask: does it really matter? We can't help but pity the improperly dressed man and question the king's severe punishment. After all, the king's servants had urged him to come to the banquet: even though he was at the edge of town, on the fringes of society, they still wanted him to join them. Should a man like this be expected to dress fancifully? And should the king really have cared so much about what his guests were wearing, as long as they came to the party?

Isn't God's banquet, the wedding of the Lamb and the church ... isn't the Kingdom of God ... about grace? Are we not meant to come "just as we are?"

When we hurl these questions at Matthew's Gospel, an uncomfortable truth stares back at us: There is more than one way to respond unworthily to God's gracious invitation and more than one way to dismiss the Kingdom of God.

This is where my fundamentalist friends would probably chime in, telling us that the wedding garment represents the blood of Christ, the vestment of salvation.

God's chief desire, I bet they would say, is to gather worthy guests for the Son's banquet. The one who arrives without the right clothes, without repentance and righteousness, is just as unworthy as s/he who rejects the king's invitation outright.

And, you know something? Maybe they're right!

Isaiah 61:10 uses the clothing image beautifully in the context of its message: "I will greatly rejoice in the LORD, my whole being shall exult in my God; for he has clothed me with the garments of salvation, he has covered me with the robe of righteousness, as a bridegroom decks himself with a garland, and as a bride adorns herself with her jewels."

Despite their tattered clothing, others at this wedding understood the nature of the king's invitation. Honored by the summons to celebrate with him, they took time to find something to wear, maybe even begging or borrowing to do so. Doubtless, some still looked like people off the streets; but they rejoiced with royalty because they came prepared to celebrate with their lord at the banquet.

Yet this one guest and his clothes betrayed his indifference to the king. No, it's more than indifference ... it's sheer contempt. He is there eating the food, drinking the wine, enjoying all the mirth and merriment. But he is just as bad, some would say, as those who rebuffed the king's rule with a last-minute refusal ... maybe even worse. He is declining to celebrate with the king and does so while standing in the king's presence!

And here then, my friends, is the difficulty: If we're honest with ourselves, we'd agree that we sympathize with the improperly dressed man, because we identify with his easy-going frivolity.

We know God's grace is wide and welcoming. We know God's generosity is endless and that God's mercy endures forever. Why not just relax and enjoy the benefits of the Kingdom? Why not come to God's party just as we are, rather than worry about wearing robes and cloaking ourselves with a banner of righteousness and a covering for our sins?

The answer, I believe, is in the parable's message: The wedding garment is our tribute to the king. Without it, we are unworthy wedding crashers, fit more for a trash-lined alley. Because, in this banquet of God, our clothing reflects our understanding of the celebration. What we wear reveals that we have accepted the invitation and are willing to join the king in his joy.

Yes, God invites us to come to the wedding just as we are; the invitation is a free gift of grace. But we're also expected to remember who invited us and why we are there ... which means that we should dress accordingly and act appropriately.

This passage confronts us with the paradox of God's free invitation to the banquet with no strings attached and God's requirement of "putting on" something appropriate to that calling. It's the essential dynamic tugging between grace and works of our faith as expressed through our deeds.

As with all paradoxes, both are true and concentrating only on one is unhealthy. The trick is learning to manage the two extremes, to wear the right clothes and accessories.

Let's not forget that this passage, as written, was directed at the Jews of Matthew's time. But what about today? Is there some additional "take-away" we can glean from the Scripture?

Perhaps it's something as simple as stated by motivational speaker Wayne Dyer and amplified here: "When you change the way you look at things, the things that you look at change … and you change the way you look."

Then again, maybe it means that our church bells continue to ring, calling many to worship and follow the Lord; however, it's no longer the choir robes, shawls, or outerwear garments that matter, but the fruit of the Spirit that signals who we are and what we're wearing to the Lamb's wedding?

After all, Matthew 7:16 says that, "by their fruits, you shall know them." Maybe love, joy, peace, forbearance, kindness, goodness, faithfulness, gentleness and self-control – the gifts of the Spirit that Paul mentions in Galatians – are the garments that now distinguish us from being just plain ordinary.

In the end, I submit, it won't really matter whether we're in church or at a wedding, but that we've changed our clothing and come clean with the Lord!

The wedding banquet anecdote contextually unmasks the threefold meaning of its message as conveyed by its content (the "facts" of what happened in this story without any implications or interpretation); its medium (a parable told by Jesus); and its persons (the invited guest/s, the king, and the king's son).

According to the Facebook Gospel, the message we ascribe to any given scripture will be a measure of whether we believe its focus is to be on the content, medium, or person(s) involved.

A BIGGER AND BETTER GOD

Much as the Talmud – rabbinic commentaries and interpretations of the Torah (Old Testament) – has, in large measure, supplanted the Hebrew Testament scriptures as the main guiding principles of Judaism, so, too, have the other books of the Christian Testament – especially those of Pauline doctrine – overshadowed the Gospels ... the Gospel message of Jesus Christ!

For Christians to truly understand the Kingdom of God, perhaps we must refrain from the temptation to believe commentary extrinsic to the Christ's message: what He said (and didn't say), what He did (and didn't do).

By so doing, historical dogma and traditional doctrines promulgated by Jewish and Christian leaders can be questioned. On Facebook, especially, they are!

(Yet despite the current penchant for "crowd-sharing" and its assumption that truth must be evident when so many people converge and converse on whatever the theme or purpose, let's not forget that – given what pushes and pulls them – crowds can also be wrong. Remember how the crowd chanted, "Crucify him! Crucify him!"?)

As the late Steve Jobs put it, "Don't let the noise of other people's opinions drown out your own inner voice."

Yes, I found that quote posted on Facebook, too.

Anyway …

Have you ever met someone who questions your beliefs, assumes that you can't possibly really believe in God because of your "lifestyle," and, worse, insinuates or declares without reservation that, "God couldn't — wouldn't — love you because …"????

Silly questions, huh?

What they're saying, in effect, is that their God isn't big enough for you or me.

Someone I know, a Seventh Day Adventist, had been e-mailing me Bible verses, all the "usual suspects" plus Genesis 1:27 ("So God created man in his image – male and female he created them") and Genesis 2:24 ("For this reason, a man will leave his father and mother and be united to his wife").

Apart from not particularly agreeing with the translation, I found myself getting a bit irritated by her insistence on setting me straight.

After asking why she had felt compelled to send me these Scriptures and being told that she and her religion disagreed about the ability of two men to truly love each other and be blessed by God, I gently made my case.

"You know, Elena, I grew up Jewish," I began, relating to her beliefs about worshipping on Saturdays and keeping kosher in diet.

"Be that as it may," I continued, "the God I now believe in and seek to serve is less concerned about the letters of the law you're so focused on than on us loving God and our neighbors … whosoever they may be."

I certainly don't mean to pick on Seventh Day Adventists—every religion, every denomination, every Bible believer, tends to place limits on what's acceptable to God and what's not.

Some common examples:

✞ The Bible, the King James version at that, is the infallible word of God.

✞ We must use wine/not grape juice for communion … or, we must use grape juice/not wine.

✞ You're not "saved" unless you've answered an altar call, been baptized … and/or been filled by the Holy Spirit—as evidenced by speaking in tongues.

✞ Some people are pre-destined to be "saved" … God purposely excludes others. Or, God loves us unconditionally vs. God loves us when or if …

✞ If you believe the Bible and faithfully confess what it says, but the expected blessing doesn't come to you, the problem is your lack of faith.

✞ We should have poisonous snakes at worship services because the Gospel of Mark says real believers will be able to handle them without any harm.

Because we're human, all of us tend to limit God and make the Sacred Essence smaller to ourselves, as well as to others.

But if we believe that Jesus most correctly embraces the sacred word and holy will of God, then, as Christians – followers of the Christ's teachings – we must reexamine the confines of our beliefs and ask ourselves, "What did Jesus say about this? What didn't he say? How did he act or react?"

Take, for example, Jesus' reaction to same-sex love and relationships.

Rather the brow-beat those same old clobber verses, let's take a look at the story of Cornelius the Centurion.

Cornelius the Centurion

In Acts 10:34-43, Peter announces that God's amazing grace is on the move, breaking down traditional boundaries and barriers between the Jews and the nations (gentiles).

Through his encounter with Cornelius, Peter comes to realize that "God shows no partiality" ... in every nation (whether geographical, cultural, or social), anyone who reveres God and does what is right is accepted by God.

WOW! God shows no partiality.

Think about how that statement challenges and undermines our tendency to harness God to the comfortable categories of our own religion or religious beliefs.

Consider Cornelius: Why might God have chosen him and his household to be the first gentile converts to Christianity?

From the scriptures above, we know that he's a centurion, a notable leader of Roman soldiers. He's described as "God-fearing," someone who loves the Lord, prays regularly, and one who helps the poor. We're told that he even built a synagogue for the Jews. We're also informed that he lives in Caesaria, was part of the Italian regiment, and that his entire "household" – kinfolk, friends, and servants – worshipped God.

Given the time, place, and Cornelius's position, this was truly radical!

Even more radical is that Cornelius, I believe, is the same man referred to either as "a centurion" or "the centurion" whom we've met elsewhere in the Gospels.

In Matthew and Luke, we're told that, at the crucifixion of Jesus, "When the centurion and others keeping watch over Jesus saw ... what took place, they were filled with awe and said, 'Truly this was the Son of God!'" (Matthew 27:54). Luke (23:47) adds, "When the centurion saw what had taken place, he praised God and said, 'Certainly this man was innocent!'"

I sincerely believe this centurion was Cornelius, paying his last respects to the blessed man and teacher who, earlier, had healed his servant.

In my humble opinion, the centurion we're introduced to in Matthew and Luke is Cornelius. Remember the story about the centurion who sought Jesus to heal his servant "who was <u>dear</u> to him?"

Examine how this story is told in Luke 7:1-10 of the World English Bible:

> "After he had finished speaking in the hearing of the people, he entered into Capernaum. A certain centurion's servant, who was dear to him, was sick and at the point of death. When he heard about Jesus, he sent to him elders of the Jews, asking him to come and save his servant. When they came to Jesus, they begged him earnestly, saying, "He is worthy for you to do this for him, for he loves our nation, and he built our synagogue for us." Jesus went with them. When he was now not far from the house, the centurion sent friends to him, saying to him, "Lord, don't trouble yourself, for I am not worthy for you to come under my roof. Therefore I didn't even think myself worthy to come to you; but say the word, and my servant will be healed. For I also am a man placed under authority, having under myself soldiers. I tell this one, 'Go!' and he goes; and to another, 'Come!' and he comes; and to my servant, 'Do this,' and he does it." When Jesus

heard these things, he marveled at him, and turned and said to the multitude who followed him, "I tell you, I have not found so great faith, no, not in Israel." Those who were sent, returning to the house, found that the servant who had been sick was well."

The story told in Matthew's Gospel is pretty much the same ... except that the centurion, himself, approaches Jesus rather than sending the elders of the Jews in his behalf.

In either case, many people – including Bible scholars who have analyzed the words "dear to him" in this passage – believe there was a very special relationship, a deep, loving relationship, between the centurion and his servant. I believe it was this special, same-sex love that touched Jesus' heart and motivated him to reach out and heal the man's servant. And to accept – even bless! – the relationship between the centurion and his servant.

If you were an exalted soldier of rank and power, respected by your own people, would you beseech help from a wandering rabbi of a foreign religion for a mere servant of yours? Would you forsake your own god or gods and humble yourself in front of the supposedly ignorant natives who were your subjects, just to cure someone who worked for you?

Not likely. Not if you were a Roman centurion. You would not, could not, risk the ridicule ... even if you were in love with another man, as was often the custom among Roman men such as this at the time.

As the centurion made his way toward Jesus, I'm sure he was concerned that Jesus, like other Jewish rabbis, would condemn his "dear" relationship. But he probably decided that if Jesus was able to heal his beloved, he was also able to see through any lies or deception.

In response to the centurion's love and his honesty, Jesus said without reservation: "Then I will come and heal him."

The centurion replied there is no need, that Jesus' word was sufficient.

Instead of Jesus saying, "he is healed ... go and sin no more," as he did to the adulterous woman, he said, "I have not found faith this great anywhere in Israel," and held Cornelius up as a man of true faith.

It's apparent to me that the Lord was already working in Cornelius' life, preparing him for the events which would occur to him and his household in Acts chapter ten.

For centuries, the church has insisted that loving, homosexual people are nowhere to be found in the Bible and, certainly, never presented in a positive light. Many Christians refuse to believe that God would include a positive story about a manly centurion who loves another person of the same sex.

But I believe that our Creator has revealed another dimension, even a new dispensation, to what it means to be loved, accepted, and affirmed by God.

"The world has watched Christian rhetoric used to preserve our culture and the sanctification of capitalist greed. We have allowed the Christian religion to become a captive horde of Bible-worshiping, homophobic, fundamentalist bullies who have naïve answers for all of life's deepest ills," declares Christians Tired of Being Represented, a Facebook group with more than 71,000 members (and growing!) at the time this book was being written. "The true message of Jesus Christ has been hijacked by egocentric arrogance. This is not what Christianity should be identified with. Therefore, we believe that it is our duty and obligation to provide a safe place for those who disagree with the extreme Fundamentalist Christian; for those who have escaped fundamentalism and are in the process of recovery from it."

A wild and winsome force, God's love can win over the hearts of rigid and exclusionary Christians, just as it won over centurions like Cornelius. It says, "Bah-humbug" to the conventional categories of who's deemed "in" and who's cast "out." It eats with sinners, washes the feet of ordinary men, associates with prostitutes and other people of ill repute, and upholds loving one's enemies as a commanding new norm.

Yet we continue our attempts to control the Almighty, holding God hostage within predetermined limits.

Let's be cautious about attempting to capture and control the parameters by which we define God who, historically, always has eluded human attempts to be restricted, restrained, or retained.

When all is said and done, our gods are too small; God is bigger than any and all of our beliefs. Perhaps we worship the God of our interpretation and imagination. Certainly, our theology determines the God we worship. I think all people are a reflection of God and conclude that God is too big and diverse for us ever to comprehend, really.

Rather than argue or debate the religious fundamentalists over their select agenda of Bible verses and interpretations, I now simply say to them: "My God is bigger – and better – than that!"

ELIZABETH'S STORY: AMAZING GRACE!

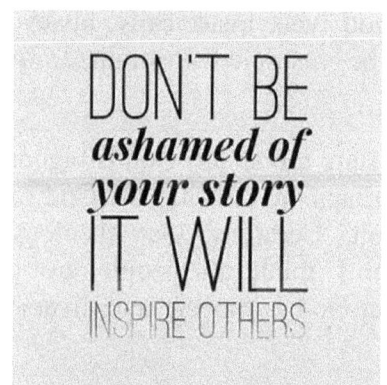

Gender expectations and Bible beliefs extend well beyond same-sex relationships. Women, especially, are often belittled or compromised by our churches, silently conspiring to relegate them to second-class citizenship.

"The truth is that male religious leaders have had – and still have – an option to interpret holy teachings either to exalt or subjugate women. They have, for their own selfish ends, overwhelmingly chosen the latter. Their continuing choice provides the foundation or justification for much of the pervasive persecution and abuse of women throughout the world," insisted former U.S. President Jimmy Carter in "Losing My Religion for Equality," a column he wrote for *Women's Press* in January 2013 which quickly appeared all over Facebook.

Thanks largely to Paul's teachings (whether taken out of context or not), the church traditionally has held women "in their place" … behind men.

Sure there are biblical heroines: Ruth, Esther, Rahab, Bathsheba, Miriam, Deborah, Priscilla, and Mary Magdalene – among many others – all have their strengths (and weaknesses). Especially in the Roman Catholic Church, there is nobody quite so highly revered and venerated as Mary, mother of Jesus.

Elizabeth's story tends to be eclipsed by Mary's, since it's hard not to focus on a virgin birth. But Elizabeth has a miraculous birth as well, pregnant well beyond the normal and expected time to have children.

Let's take a look at Elizabeth's life.

Living in one of the hill towns of Judea, Elizabeth and her husband, Zechariah, were holy people: righteous in the sight of God, observing all the Lord's commands and decrees blamelessly (Luke 1:6). While her childlessness could have been grounds for divorce if Zechariah wanted it, their love was such that he accepted her being barren ... although we now know their fertility problem might have been his!

A descendant of the priestly line of Aaron, Elizabeth and Zechariah were old—she well past the child-bearing years. Yet she conceived. According to the biblical text, an angel (Gabriel) told Zechariah the news while the old man was performing his priestly duties in the Jerusalem Temple. Because Zechariah didn't believe the angel's pronouncement, he was rendered mute for a time.

Elizabeth's response to her miraculous pregnancy was quite different from her husband's: hiding herself for five months and acknowledging God for taking away her disgrace among the people (Luke 1:25).

Beginning with Sarah early in Genesis, the inability to bear a child is a common theme in the Bible—often despite outstanding character references. In ancient times, barrenness was considered a disgrace. But time and again, we see these women having great faith in God, who ultimately blesses them with a child or children.

Barren, however, means more than just infertile; it means unproductive, unattractive, unfruitful, dull, empty, devoid, lacking, bereft.

At one time or another – maybe even many times! –like Elizabeth, we feel barren ... unproductive ... empty ... lacking ... or bereft. Sometimes, God has reasons for not answering our prayers—or not answering them when or how we want them to be answered. Being human, it's hard to wait ... and wait ... and wait for our prayers to be answered.

Oh, I could tell you to do like Elizabeth: Go about your daily life and business, loving the people God has placed in your life while never giving up your faith or hope. That would have been a fine and fitting ending to this story.

But the more I read about Elizabeth, the more I find myself riveted on her words of redemption, in Luke 1:25: "The Lord has done this for me ... he has shown his favor and taken away my disgrace among the people."

Think about these words, will you? Not only did Elizabeth do nothing wrong, we're told she did everything right. Right from the beginning, we're informed she was "blameless" in front of the Lord.

Yet her society judged her to be shameful, disgraceful, lacking in God's grace ... as if it were her fault that she hadn't conceived and given birth to children as expected.

Don't we feel that way, too, sometimes because we don't exactly conform to society's norms and expectations?

"What did I do to deserve this?" we ask ourselves. "Why was I created this way? What should I do now to feel better about myself ... and not so barren or empty?"

When I began to come to grips with my own identity, I already knew that I didn't make myself this way ... nor did I believe that my environment or other people caused me to become the person I am now. I regretted that I wasn't like everyone else. It certainly wasn't easy to make believe, hide in the closet, and try to deny the person I was meant to be.

Yet because society deemed it wrong, shameful, disgraceful, with an ugly stigma attached to it, I – like Elizabeth – felt barren ... empty ... and void.

I remember going to a Coming Out Group led by a Christian counselor named Paul. "BUT ... how do I reconcile my sexuality with all those verses in the Bible?" I asked him. He just smiled oh-so-sweetly and told me that the God he worships loves him ... just as he is ... and that – no matter what other people might tell me or what could be taken out of context from the Scriptures – that it's really all about grace.

Amazing grace!

It's got nothing to do with what we do or don't do that earns us God's love and acceptance. It's not about rules, regulations, and restrictions that lead to heavenly rewards or rejection.

Nope, it's all about grace. Even now, I'm just coming to understand and accept this astounding truth.

Being loved by someone I deeply love in return certainly has helped me to feel somewhat better about myself ... but I still was alone, if not so lonely anymore.

It wasn't until I met God more intimately – not someone else's idea of God – and spent time in God's presence that I began to truly feel better about being myself ... and not quite so empty. God's grace and my belief that God purposefully created me to be exactly the person I am has turned my life around—blessing me and making me barren no more.

Listen, again, to the redeeming words of Elizabeth as found in Luke 1:25:

"The Lord has done this for me ... he has shown his favor ... and taken away my disgrace among the people."

That's a lesson we can live with and truly believe.

In the Gospel according to Facebook, communities of spiritual people hitherto considered outcasts and nonconformists by conventional Christianity are discovering there's no shame in being different or disgrace for believing differently. They're sharing their stories publicly; sometimes just with friends and other times "going viral" with everyone who's interested.

Their spirituality has turned The Gospel according to Facebook into something quite relevant, personal, and timely.

Peering into an online prism reflecting Jesus surrounded by his own band of strangers and misfits, we are comforted by the concern and consideration of others seeking travel companions along our digital highways and byways.

It is not good to be alone. So, regardless of where we are along the way, it's welcoming to share a message of the sacred that bespeaks grace.

In its own way, it's communion.

The Lord God has taken away our disgrace.

EUNUCHS AND GENDER IDENTITY

Imagine if you were a special "type" of person ... someone who belonged to what might be called a sexual minority ... a person who would be conveniently used by others when your special gifts and talented were needed.

Yet, although you were good-natured, attractive, talented, and trustworthy, you had no civil rights or legal standing whatsoever.

Not too hard to imagine, huh?

Lots of Facebook people can, which is why they turn to this social medium to be in community with others who understand what it's like to feel this way. They seek not just acceptance, but affirmation that they're loved by God.

Similarly, a group of people in the Bible known as "eunuchs" faced comparable predicaments and banishment from the Kingdom of God ... until Jesus changed the rules of inclusion.

Eunuch.

Even the name, itself, sounds strange. Be that as it may, some scholars say there upwards of 40 Old Testament verses containing a word – in Hebrew, Greek or Aramaic – used to mean "eunuch," while, in at least two New Testament passages, eunuchs are at the heart of the message.

What, exactly, is a eunuch? Simple: A eunuch is someone who has no physical attraction to people of the opposite sex. Back in the Bible, eunuchs didn't have sex with women and they didn't have children. Since they had no children, they had no vested interest in leaving a fortune to the next generation. So they had no reason to be corrupt or seek advantage for their own offspring.

Eunuchs were incapacitated for marriage or for begetting children.

Some people were born that way. Others were made that way (surgically) in order to serve their masters. Still others chose to deny themselves and be celibate in order to focus entirely on God.

Translated to English, eunuch means "keeper of the bed chamber" or "overseer of the household." Put another way, a eunuch was an "emasculated man." Quite a few historians believe that eunuchs were homosexuals.

Evidently, people living thousands of years ago all across Europe and Asia acknowledged a certain category of men as different from the norm. Their difference consisted in the fact that they had no sex drive toward women and that difference was conceived of as natural and inborn.

(We know, too, of ancient cultures where there were women who, by nature, had no lust for men. Does the island of "Lesbos" ring a bell?)

The ancient Hebrews didn't practice castration. The Law excluded eunuchs from public worship, partly because self-mutilation was often performed in honor of a heathen god and partly because any maimed creature was deemed unfit for the service of Yahweh. That ban, however, was later removed. The kings of Israel and Judah often followed their royal neighbors in employing eunuchs as guardians of the harem and other official posts.

Eunuchs were common in other cultures featured in the Bible. Remember Potiphar, who managed the household of a high-ranking official in Pharaoh's court? He was a eunuch. Maybe that explains why the official's wife made a play, instead, for Joseph, he of the coat of many colors. Joseph tried to escape and left the woman holding his garment but that, my friends, is another story.

Eunuchs were trusted around women who were married since they weren't a threat in committing adultery with another man's wife or engaging in sex with a household of women.

Both boys and girls were sold into slavery as eunuchs by their parents to give their children a better life or to provide for the rest of the family.

Eunuchs could be extremely beautiful and attractive. Some say that Daniel – along with his friends Shadrach, Meschach, and Abednego – were virile and handsome men who were castrated before being banished into captivity by the Babylonians and sent to serve Nebuchadnezzar. First century historian Josephus asserts that Daniel and his three friends were made eunuchs. Even before that, the writer of 2 Kings 20:18 predicts: "And some of your descendants, your own flesh and blood that will be born to you, will be taken away and they will become eunuchs in the palace of the king of Babylon."

While in exile, Queen Esther – the wife of Persian King Xerxes – had a eunuch assigned to serve her personal needs, showing that in this time period it was common for such women to be attended by men who didn't pose a sexual threat. According to the Book of Esther (1:10), the king had seven eunuchs who served him.

The New Testament also refers to eunuchs. Candace, Queen of the Ethiopians, sent one of her eunuchs to Jerusalem to worship Yahweh, God of the Hebrews. As the eunuch was drawing close to Jerusalem, the Apostle Phillip, one of the leaders in the early Christian church, was sent by God to explain and preach the Gospel to him. But I'm getting a bit ahead of myself here. (You can read the entire story in Acts 8:26-31.)

Ironically, some could say that the Apostle Paul was a eunuch in that he remained single and celibate to fully concentrate on his mission for Christ.

What's really important here is the idea that even a eunuch could be baptized, draw close to God, and become part of God's family. I believe this reaffirms the impartiality of God.

"Whoever believes," says the scripture ... and that includes eunuchs.

Which brings us to what Jesus had to say about these extraordinary people. Let's take a look at Matthew 19:8-12, where Jesus and his disciples are discussing marriage and divorce, and conditions under which it is permissible to divorce:

> "Jesus replied, 'Moses permitted you to divorce your wives because your hearts were hard. But it was not this way from the beginning. I tell you that anyone who divorces his wife, except for marital unfaithfulness, and marries another woman commits adultery.' The disciples said to him, 'If this is the situation between a husband and wife, it is better not to marry.' Jesus replied, 'Not everyone can accept this word, but only those to whom it has been given. For some are eunuchs because they were born that way; others were made that way by men; and others have renounced marriage because of the kingdom of heaven. The one who can accept this should accept it.'"

In this context, Jesus is saying that some people aren't suitable for marriage. His reasons are lumped together under the category of being a eunuch. The Lord himself has expanded the meaning of eunuch to include those who are unmarried for a variety of reasons. Some were made this way by others. Some were born this way, unable to get married because they have no natural instinct or inclination to have sexual relations with a mate of the opposite sex.

It is highly unlikely that Jesus is referring to heterosexual, but impotent males ... or castrated ones, for that matter ... when he talks about eunuchs.

Castrated and impotent men still can be attracted to women. A eunuch is a man who can't reproduce, not necessarily a man who isn't sexual. Some men were castrated specifically so they could stay young and pretty and be sexual with other men.

We've all heard the joke about the pamphlet entitled, "What Jesus Said about Homosexuality." Open it up and it's blank. Of course, that's true. Jesus never mentioned homosexuality, per se.

But as knowing and wise as Jesus was – or, as the fundamentalists like to say, "Jesus Christ is the same yesterday, today and forever" (Hebrews 13:8) – wouldn't you think He'd know that there would one day be a terrible problem in his church, in Christianity, and in culture over homosexuality, gay rights, and same-sex marriage? Then, why didn't he say anything specific?

According to the Facebook Gospel, I believe he did. In Matthew 19:12.

Jesus said, "Let the one who can accept this accept it." Not everyone can accept this. So, I have to wonder: Is Jesus talking to us, preaching to the choir? Or is he talking about others in his church who need to understand and accept what he's saying here about eunuchs ... about those of us who don't conform to society's norms about gender?

> For this is what the Lord says: "To the eunuchs who keep my Sabbaths, who choose what pleases me and hold fast to my covenant—to them I will give within my temple and its walls a memorial and a name better than sons and daughters. I will give

them an everlasting name that will endure forever" (Isaiah 56:4-5).

Due to one of those damning Deuteronomy verses (23:1): "No one who has been emasculated by crushing or cutting may enter the assembly of the Lord," eunuchs were foreigners to God's temple when Isaiah made this prophecy.

But Isaiah here states that God will wipe away the bonds of the Mosaic Law through love, mercy, and grace.

It is, therefore, very clear that eunuchs not only have a place in heaven, but are given an everlasting "name better than sons and daughters."

Cut off from God by established religion, those who choose to please and be in covenant with the Lord will be called by a name that will endure forever.

Can it get any better than that?

Just imagine the number of *Likes* and shares this message would receive if posted on Facebook!

SOCIAL JUSTICE AND THE KINGDOM OF GOD

The prophetic voices at the heart of our faith speak not only of promises of God's blessings, but warnings of God's judgment. We would do well to heed them, too. Biblical Israel aspired to attain a vision in which all people were recognized as reflections of God's image—each person of equal worth and dignity.

Today, the difference between Christian social justice and the world's is a matter not just of goodwill but free will, not of exclusion but inclusion.

Social justice is at the very core of Jesus' teachings. In his parable about the sheep and the goats, Jesus is quite clear about his concept of social justice:

> "When the Son of Man comes in his glory, and all the angels with him, he will sit on his glorious throne. All the nations will be gathered before him, and he will separate the people one from another as a shepherd separates the sheep from the goats. He will put the sheep on his right and the goats on his left. Then the King will say to those on his right, 'Come, you who are blessed by my Father; take your inheritance, the kingdom

prepared for you since the creation of the world. For I was hungry and you gave me something to eat, I was thirsty and you gave me something to drink, I was a stranger and you invited me in, I needed clothes and you clothed me, I was sick and you looked after me, I was in prison and you came to visit me.' Then the righteous will answer him, 'Lord, when did we see you hungry and feed you, or thirsty and give you something to drink? When did we see you a stranger and invite you in, or needing clothes and clothe you? When did we see you sick or in prison and go to visit you?' The King will reply, 'Truly I tell you, whatever you did for one of the least of these brothers and sisters of mine, you did for me.' Then he will say to those on his left, 'Depart from me, you who are cursed, into the eternal fire prepared for the devil and his angels. For I was hungry and you gave me nothing to eat, I was thirsty and you gave me nothing to drink, I was a stranger and you did not invite me in, I needed clothes and you did not clothe me, I was sick and in prison and you did not look after me.' They also will answer, 'Lord, when did we see you hungry or thirsty or a stranger or needing clothes or sick or in prison, and did not help you?' He will reply, 'Truly I tell you, whatever you did not do for one of the least of these, you did not do for me.'" (Matthew 25: 31-45)

Clearly, what we don't do for the least among us – the poor, the destitute, the infirm, the sick, the incarcerated, the sexual minorities, the victims of war and politics – we aren't doing for Jesus, either.

People who share the Facebook Gospel, much like those who follow the more traditional, canonical Gospels, tend to believe and agree about this principle of social justice in the Kingdom of God.

"If you want peace, work for justice," intoned Pope Paul VI.

Depending on our political orientation and/or religious values – conservative, fundamental, liberal, progressive, fiscally conservative but socially progressive – we interpret our stewardship responsibilities quite differently.

Those who follow the Gospel according to Facebook are usually more open-minded and magnanimous than mainstream Bible literalists, believing that we are stewards of God's creation, responsible to care for and sustain it.

Are we, therefore, our brother's keeper? Yes. And our sister's, the stranger's, a neighbor's and an enemy's, if we are to take what Jesus says at face value.

There's an interesting choice of words in Micah 6:8, "What does the Lord require of you but to do justice, love mercy, and walk humbly with your God?"

The translation and emphatic differences are fascinating: We are to <u>do</u> justice; <u>love</u> mercy; and <u>walk</u> humbly with God.

I pretty much understand the requirement to walk humbly with God. Humility means acknowledging that we don't have all the answers. We walk humbly with God because we know that we may well be wrong ... even about the things we're surely convinced we're right about. I'm not always good at it, but, conceptually at least, I think I understand humility, of walking humbly with God.

Similarly, I believe that many of our hearts are filled with compassion and mercy for the hurts of others. We want to help, to "give alms" to the poor, as the church used to call it: food for the hungry ... clothing to those without ... our time and resources to support the basic needs of others, especially those in causes that particularly touch us personally.

While it's our compassion and love of God that prompt us to mercy, it seems that being merciful is more something we <u>do</u> than we love.

Curious, isn't it?

The Scripture doesn't say to "do mercy," which we all can understand; nor does it say we are "to be" merciful, something we also can comprehend.

Surely, it is a divine requirement to practice doing mercy because, as someone once said, an eye for an eye leaves everyone blind in the end.

Yet God very clearly commands us to <u>do</u> justice.

Why? What's the real difference – if any – between justice and mercy? Where does one end and the other begin?

For me, that used to be an easy distinction: The Old Testament was filled with God's judgment and justice, I believed; the New Covenant focused on God's grace, love, and mercy.

But I no longer believe it's as simple or clear-cut as that, since both the Old Testament and the New give evidence of God's mercy <u>and</u> God's justice.

Asked about the most important commandment, Jesus said the first commandment, to "Love the Lord your God with all of your heart, and soul, and mind, and might," along with the second commandment, to "love your neighbor as yourself," accurately summed up all of the Law and the Prophets.

Loving God with all my heart and soul speaks to me of mercy, while loving God with all of my mind and my might makes me think more about justice. Add loving our neighbors as ourselves to this mix and we've got a potent formula for both mercy and justice.

Ahhhhhhhhhhhhh … but, again, what's the difference between them?

And, in terms of the Facebook Gospel and the heart of Christianity, what does it mean that we are to <u>do</u> justice?

You know, a really simple way of looking at the distinction is captured in an old saying that's more rational than Scriptural: "Give a man a fish and you've fed him for a day; teach a man to fish and you'll feed him for a lifetime."

<u>Give him</u> and you're showing mercy; <u>teach him</u> and you're practicing justice.

"Faith-based charity provides crumbs from the table," said Bill Moyers, "while faith-based justice offers a place at the table."

Unfortunately, too often we tend to substitute mercy for justice. Justice is what our world would be like if God really were our King and the world's rulers, governments, and rich principalities weren't calling the shots.

The New Covenant and the heart of Christianity, inherently, are about two primary changes: one personal, the other political.

"Thy Kingdom come …" Jesus taught us to beseech in the Lord's Prayer.

Not family of God, or people of God. Not churches of God, congregations or assemblies, pastors and priests, elders and laypersons of God. But the <u>Kingdom</u> of God! Jesus purposefully chose political terminology in allegories to which the people of his time could relate.

They were hungry, so He fed them; they hurt, so he healed them; as serfs and servants, they owed great debts to their masters, so Jesus asked that their debts be forgiven; they were in bondage, so Jesus prayed they'd be set free.

Interesting, isn't it, in terms of the Gospel message, that there's at once such a practical and prayerful dimension to Jesus?

God hates injustice, especially when it is "systemic" – embedded in the system itself, against which we have little recourse but to find ourselves or others victimized, marginalized, and taken advantage of.

Unfortunately, this great country of ours has a history of injustice.

Our forefathers stole the land we're living on from Native Americans, forcing them into concentration camps we call "reservations." These *shtetls,* as they'd be referred to in Yiddish, come up pitifully short when compared to our own gated communities. And to compensate them for these inequities, what do we give the Indian people? The right to make tax-free money from gambling, smoking, and drinking on their premises!

African-Americans and people of color suffered horribly at the hands of their slave-driving masters and mistresses. The U.S. Constitution deemed black people to be worth just three-fifths of a white person. That battle for equal rights still hasn't ended. Just listen to what's whispered when certain "good, Christian folks" talk secretly among themselves.

Women, too, were denied their essential rights. While it wasn't until 1920 that females were finally "granted" the right to vote, let's not forget that our Pharisaical friend, the Apostle Paul, urged women to be quiet and submissive, and to ask their husbands – or other men – when they needed or wanted to say something on their own behalf.

Whether mentally or physically challenged, the handicapped have suffered grave injustices by an unwelcoming, unaccommodating system of physical barriers and unforgiving expectations ... until the ADA was enacted.

And, always, the poor remain here dwelling among us.

Ten years ago, our socioeconomics divided this country according to our riches: we were upper class, middle class, and lower class ... with respective derogatory implications about our social worth as well as our finances. Today, that's no longer the case. While we're still a three-class country, it's now the haves, the used-to-haves, and the have-nots!

Immigrants whom we had welcomed with outstretched hands and a beacon of liberty, arrived on our shores to be greeted by these words from The New Colossus, a sonnet by Emma Lazarus engraved in 1903 on a bronze plaque mounted inside the Statue of Liberty:

> *Not like the brazen giant of Greek fame,*
> *With conquering limbs astride from land to land;*
> *Here at our sea-washed, sunset gates shall stand*
> *A mighty woman with a torch, whose flame*
> *Is the imprisoned lightning, and her name*
> *Mother of Exiles. From her beacon-hand*
> *Glows world-wide welcome; her mild eyes command*
> *The air-bridged harbor that twin cities frame.*
> *"Keep, ancient lands, your storied pomp!" cries she*
> *With silent lips. "Give me your tired, your poor,*
> *Your huddled masses yearning to breathe free,*
> *The wretched refuse of your teeming shore.*
> *Send these, the homeless, tempest-tost to me,*
> *I lift my lamp beside the golden door!"*

And today? Do we still believe and echo these words? E Pluribus Unum. Out of many, one?

And then, of course, there are our sexual minorities. The last socially acceptable bias and bigotry, still scorned, punished, and damned by the religious establishment and civil authorities. Inalienable rights of life, liberty, and the pursuit of happiness? Yeah, right! Not only are LGBT people still treated as second class citizens in this country, but too many municipalities categorically exclude them from discriminatory prejudice and practices against which everyone <u>else</u> is protected.

Today, as the largest sovereign superpower, we employ our resources to strike, preemptively, against those we suppose could challenge us … while withholding food, humanitarian help, aid, and justice to punish people and places that reject our vision or values in building their nations according to our self-serving goals or expectations. In our own homeland, people are starving, dying without roofs over their heads, losing their last shreds of dignity as Atlas shrugs and looks beyond them, to fund pork for its favored sons and daughters while we waste precious resources denying truths and jockeying for yet even more power.

"When the power of love overcomes the love of power, the world will know peace," said American singer-songwriter Jimi Hendrix.

But justice isn't just about power and punishment; it's about fairness.

A just society is a society that treats all of its citizens alike. We in the United States historically have treated one segment of our population differently than another. That, brothers and sisters, is social injustice.

What's worse, we continue to do so.

The struggle for civil rights has become a quest for <u>human</u> rights, for a society that treats all of its members with the same degree of fairness.

God's justice calls for the fair treatment of all creation—not just of mankind, but of the earth, and sea, and skies above, and everything that lives among us. "It is good," said the Lord, when considering each and every act of creation.

If only we could say and believe as well.

"Sometimes I would like to ask God why He allows poverty, suffering, and injustice, when He could do something about it.

But I'm afraid that He would ask me the same question." I wish someone could identify the author of this statement, to give credit where it's due (and render God more gender neutral). Since I can't, here are two quotes that I can attribute:

"If you are neutral in situations of injustice, you have chosen the side of the oppressor," warned Nobel Peace Prize winner Archbishop Desmond Tutu, while the Rev. Martin Luther King, Jr. reminded us that, "Injustice anywhere is a threat to justice everywhere."

The Facebook Gospel is passionate about social issues.

Many of the earliest prophets – Isaiah, Ezekiel, and Amos, among others – called loudly and often for the fair treatment of the disadvantaged.

Righteousness was one of the primary themes woven throughout the Gospel of Matthew. Among the Beatitudes which form the heart of Jesus' powerful Sermon on the Mount, we find, "Blessed are those who hunger and thirst for righteousness, for they will be filled."

That puts righteousness – an outrage and indignation over injustice – squarely in the center of Jesus' prevailing message.

Perhaps nowhere does Jesus speak as forcefully on human rights and relations as he does in the familiar parable of the sheep and the goats.

The sheep on the right will be invited to inherit God's kingdom because they fed the hungry, gave drink to the thirsty, welcomed the stranger, clothed the naked, and visited the imprisoned. Conversely, the goats on the left will hear, "Truly I tell you, just as you did not do it to one of the least of these, you did not do it to me."

So, what would Jesus say about the injustice that continues to surround us … even 2,000 years after he founded his church?

Honestly, I'm not really sure.

But I suppose he would again remind us of the powerful words he taught us to entreat God, fervently, whenever we pray:

"Thy Kingdom come, thy will be done, on earth as it is in heaven!"

THE HEART OF THE MATTER

The matter started quite simply enough: The pastor of our local United Church of Christ had agreed to officiate at a same-sex commitment ceremony sponsored and promoted by the area's tourism bureau to reach a targeted niche market in a state that had amended its constitution such that neither same-sex marriage nor civil unions would be legal or recognized. While a former governor had attempted to provide some protections to his LGBT constituents in committed relationships by enacting a "Domestic Partnership" registry with limited licenses and rights, that was also being challenged now by less-than-liberal activists who didn't want people here to have any part of certain civil liberties whatsoever.

Nonetheless, one of the state's major meccas for tourists – especially those who appreciated the arts of all kinds – decided to invite gays and lesbians in relationships to participate in a county-wide "Commit with Pride" celebration featuring special events and activities with reduced rates and culminating in a "mass" commitment ceremony.

Immediately after the local newspaper reported about the planned weekend (in print and on its Facebook page), the following letter to the editor appeared from a reader who objected to the event because of biblical reasons.

Event Goes Against the Bible

It is with a heavy heart that I write this letter, lamenting the fact that the (DCVB) Visitor's Bureau has chosen to host this event.

I find it troubling that the DCVB has taken a very strong stance on a heated social issue, just for the sake of appealing to this "niche market."

I am a disciple of Jesus Christ. To be clear, the (pastor) is not following the teachings of the Bible in performing this ceremony. My concern regarding his presence is that people will get the impression that the Bible says being gay is OK. The Bible is clear that homosexuality is wrong. I realize there are many people who do not believe in the truth of the Bible, nor are they followers of Jesus, and so they will attempt to invalidate my argument by saying it is only based on the Bible.

I would like to pose a simple question: is gravity untrue just because a person does not believe in it? There are many things about this world that are true whether you believe in them or not. Is it possible that the Bible is not also true, no matter what? I am not angry and I feel no hatred toward gays – I am called to love as Christ loved, and so that is what I try to do. I am also called to speak the truth in love, which is why I will not water down the Gospel and say that being gay is OK, nor will I spew venomous hatred as other anti-gay protesters have done.

My hope is that everyone in support of this ceremony will show respect for differing viewpoints, and consider that this may not be a step towards equality, but the decline of truth and morality.

–Bible Believer

I couldn't help but to respond, questioning some of the writer's statements, which I believed were just plain wrong. My Facebook rebuttal appeared immediately, followed in print (and online) in the paper's next issue:

DCVB, *The Scriptures and Strangers*

Responding to your letter writer (and readers) who take issue on a biblical basis with the DCVB for sponsoring a "Commit with Pride" weekend, I must admit that, although a Christian pastor, I do not believe the Bible to be the inerrant, authoritative, absolute word of God.

Indeed, God is still speaking and, while there is much sacred substance in both the Hebrew and Greek Testaments that can reveal and lead us closer to God, it is God we should worship, not the histories of given people and times: the Israelites and their covenant with God in the "Old Testament" and the emerging Christian communities in the "New Testament."

As with all literature and history, we must remember that the 66 books comprising the (Protestant) Bible were written at particular times in different language(s) and to different people(s). Over the years, what meant one thing to certain people may very well mean something else to those living in other places at other times.

Rather than argue about the intent of specific scriptures taken out of context, I ask myself instead: "What would Jesus say about this? What would the Lord do?"

Christianity has become the religion about Jesus, not of him.

Much of today's Christianity is filled with rules and regulations designed to teach that we're either going to heaven or hell, depending on whose rules and regulations we follow (or don't).

But that's not my Jesus. Nor my God.

My God is telling me to love, not hate; to include rather than exclude; to forgive, not hold grudges; neither to judge nor condemn others, but to be compassionate.

Each of us is created in God's image. And God doesn't make mistakes or create inferior, faulty products.

As we seek to love God with all our hearts and souls (minds and might) and love our neighbors as we would love ourselves, we are fulfilling the Lord's ultimate commands.

That's good enough for me.

By hosting its "Commit with Pride" weekend, the DCVB is practicing true hospitality towards today's scapegoats and strangers, the lack of which was the real sin of Sodom and Gomorrah.

–Pastor Bruce

That wasn't the end of it.

Our very public debate continued on the newspaper's editorial and Facebook pages, as messages by both of us further probed the very heart of Christianity.

She wrote:

Disagreement Is Not Hate

Dr. Joffe, I do not seek to represent the views of anyone other than myself, so please do not generalize my comments.

You have written that you do not believe the Bible to be inerrant and absolute. You suggest that those who hold the contrary view are worshiping the histories of certain people and times. I reject both your claims and assert that this is misinformation. Jesus is the Word of God made flesh (John 1:14). We worship Jesus, not "histories." As for being inerrant, you said God does not make mistakes, but also suggest that part of His Word contains mistakes.

The Bible has a proven record of veracity, and has been authenticated even by people who do not believe its claims. You say that scriptures have been taken out of context but do not say which ones, or how. "Neither fornicators, nor idolaters... nor homosexuals... shall inherit the kingdom of God" – this excerpt is 1 Corinthians 6:9. The Bible says they will not inherit the kingdom. I would welcome your comments regarding how I am taking it out of context. I would also like to suggest that instead of asking, 'What would Jesus say about this?' you can ask, 'What did Jesus already say about this?' We do not need to conjecture and wonder what he would say about anything, He already did say it when here on earth.

You also speak of rules and regulations as if people are consulting outside sources to determine if a person is going to heaven or hell. The only one who condemns a person to hell is God. Jesus said we will know a tree by its fruit (Matthew 7:16). This distinguishes a person from his or her actions. We can pass judgment on what people do, without passing judgment on them. Jesus never condoned sinful behavior – this is illustrated when He showed mercy to the woman who was caught in adultery. He said, "Neither do I condemn you, go and sin no more," (John 8:11). This is where we have gone wrong. We are condoning sin in the name of grace and love. You say the true sin of Sodom and Gomorrah was a lack of hospitality, but Genesis 19:5 refutes this claim. Desiring to "have relations" is completely unrelated to hospitality.

The dictionary distinguishes between the words disagree, hatred, love and acceptance because they are different ideas and actions. My basic premise is this: I can disagree and not hate. I can love a person and not accept the way that person lives. God certainly does want us to "love others as we love ourselves," but you define love as acceptance, and they are not the same. Being a mother, I love my son even when I do not accept his behavior. Confronting a person regarding sin is not hatred. The Bible shows the consequences for unrepentant sinners – it is wrong to know they are not saved, and tell them that they are.

–Go and Sin No More

I was about to leave well enough alone, but something within my spirit kept poking and prodding me … until I wrote and submitted what would be my last words on the subject. Or so I thought:

Amen?

(The writer's) "Disagreement Is Not Hate" begs my reply because too many people continue to be hurt by the Bible when it becomes a savage text used to judge, condemn and divide us; its many universal truths are compromised, lost in time and translation, serving only given agendas.

I guess she and I disagree about whether the Bible must be believed literally and verbatim, or if its message points to larger truths.

Do I believe that God created everything in seven days? No. Or that humanity was banished from the presence of a loving Creator because a snake bamboozled Eve into conning her husband into taking a bite of an apple? Again, no. Nonetheless, these stories point to larger and more important realities.

Instead of asking, "What would Jesus say about this?" (the writer) suggests that we ask, "What did Jesus already say about this?"

Exactly.

Unlike the story of the adulterous woman whom she cites, emphasizing that Jesus told her to "go and sin no more," the Lord said nothing – not one single word – about committed, same-sex love. In fact, many believe that in his healing of Cornelius the Centurion's beloved servant, Jesus demonstrated God is more concerned <u>that</u> we love rather than <u>whom</u> we love.

Scripture can be a two-edged sword.

If we are to zero in on one "thou shall not" (Leviticus 18:22) about men not laying with other men, we must also take just as seriously other warnings in the same section dealing with a holiness code specifically for priests: Do we wear clothing woven of two kinds of material? Do we eat meat with blood in it? Do we cut our bodies or put tattoo marks on ourselves? Do we pervert justice by showing favoritism to the 1 percent over the 99 percent?

As for much of the New Testament attributed to the Apostle Paul, do we still believe that women are to be silent in church and in full submission? That they are not to teach or assume authority over men?

The Bible isn't God; God is much bigger and greater, transcending any and all edited words.

God continues to be revealed to us along myriad sacred journeys and spiritual paths. For those of us who identify as "Christian," we find the closest expression of God in the life and teachings of Christ Jesus. Others, however, have been drawn close to the Almighty through different traditions and ways.

The Sacred One we worship is about love and forgiveness, compassion, social justice, acceptance, and affirmation. Grace is a gift, freely given, not earned by anything we do (or don't).

Why must we insist on interpreting how God will react to our humanity?

–Pastor Bruce

Our communication didn't end there; no, because we were sharing a message: the Gospel. But, according to whom? My God or hers?

Where two or more gather in the Lord's name, God is there with us.

I have no doubt that God blesses dialogue about sacred matters and spiritual journeys ... even when, ultimately, we agree to disagree.

Our conversation continued through the social media – public and private – when my critic contacted me directly:

Hello Dr. Joffe,

I understand if you choose not to respond, but I wanted to write a note in hopes that we might have a bit of dialogue. Upfront, I want you to know that I am not angry about what you wrote and this is not a reactionary email – I was sincerely hoping to learn more about your point of view. Since you are a professor, I assume you are used to being asked a lot of questions, and I would genuinely like to hear your answers, because these are things that I really do wonder about.

I am at a loss to understand why you feel I have used the Bible to forward my own agenda, but just so you are aware, I do not have one. The only thing I have tried to do through all my letters is speak the truth in love. I would like to ask one favor, though: would you explain how you arrived at your position on the Bible? When reading your letter, it seemed clear to me that you believe there are several pathways that all lead to the same Almighty God. It is also obvious that you do not trust the Bible to be inerrant, or regard it as the ultimate standard. I feel this presents a confounding problem. If we can still learn larger truths, but cannot trust the very text from which we learn them, how are we to know that they are in fact truths? My greatest concern is that a person can then pick and choose which parts of the Bible to believe, and which parts are supposedly incorrect. Wouldn't this be completely arbitrary and vary on a person-by-person basis? You say the Bible isn't God, and yet this is a direct contradiction of John 1:1-18. How does one reconcile this?

I believe the only foundation we have for understanding God is what He has revealed to us in His Word. If His Word cannot be trusted as the ultimate source about who He is, then how else are we to understand His nature without our own subjectivity coming into play? I noticed that although you said my letter "begged your response," there were multiple items to which you did not respond. The main thrust of my entire letter was the basic premise: I can disagree and not hate. I can love a person and not accept the way that person lives. Although you did not directly state this, I infer that you think this is impossible. What I find interesting is that if I follow your logic, then you must also hate me, because clearly we disagree. However, I do not believe that is actually the case. My point is that if you are disagreeing with me, while not hating me, you have proven my basic premise is completely true.

You also said that Jesus did not comment on same-sex love. The Father, the Son and the Holy Spirit are one – the Triune Godhead. The Father created Eve (woman) as the suitable mate for Adam (man), and multiple verses clearly list homosexuality as a sin. It seems that because Jesus didn't verbally make a statement, then it must be OK. You are right that we should not "zero in on one 'thou shalt not'" – I did not even mention Leviticus in my letter. Rather than zeroing in, I cited multiple books where a theme became apparent. In the case of all sexual relationships, God is concerned about who we love. His Word has much to say regarding sexual immorality, and 1 Corinthians 6:15-16 is just one example. No, Jesus never verbally said that same-sex love is wrong. He did say that a man who looks at a woman with lust has already committed adultery in his heart. This shows that, yes, God is concerned about sexual immorality. You cited the healing of the centurion's servant as possible evidence. Jesus healed a massive number of people during His public ministry, and was the friend of tax collectors. Did His miracles and His friendship mean that He agreed with how a person lived? No – He was full of grace and truth. He always called for repentance. Jesus said the tax collector who asked God to have mercy on him, a sinner, left the temple vindicated. It was the man's repentance that accomplished this – by asking for mercy, he admitted his wrongdoing. Jesus also called for us to "die to self" and live for Him. This means that there are certain aspects of ourselves, like pride, that we should suppress.

I wonder if you have heard about the infamous Westboro Baptist Church, and think that I am no different. I am being genuinely sincere when I say that I am saddened, shocked, and frustrated by their behavior. I will NEVER say that what they do is right or is representative of the teachings of Jesus Christ. Please understand that I am not the same. Besides "speak the truth in love," I also gravitate towards the scripture of Jesus being full of "grace and truth." You had referenced grace at the end of your letter, and you and I very much agree that it is a free gift from God, and that it cannot be earned. When you ended with the question "Why must we insist on interpreting how God will react to our humanity?" my initial thought was that we already know. His reaction is love. He loved us so much that, in spite of our humanity, He provided the perfect sacrifice. He knew full well that left to our own devices, it was impossible for us to save ourselves. The key is surrender to Christ – when a person claims to be Christian, but is not submitting to the lordship of Christ in how they live, this is not being a true follower. Your definition of Christian is not based on The Word – because following Jesus Christ is much more than just finding the "closest expression of God." It is a lifelong commitment that transforms the believer from inside out. I wonder how we both

> *describe ourselves as Christians, but couldn't be more opposite about what that title means. If possible, could you provide me your "definition" of Christian? I define it as voluntary submission to Jesus' authority, and adherence to the standards He set forth in His Word (with the help of the Holy Spirit).*
>
> *I realize this is pretty lengthy, and that you are a busy man, so I understand if time does not allow your response. I hope that you see I am not trying to be hateful in speaking the truth. I am only trying to do what I believe is right. I am still young (just turned 32), and I realize that I am not an expert by any stretch. But I am an honest seeker, and I firmly trust in Jesus' promise that "those who seek shall find."*
>
> *I will pray that God blesses us both with wisdom, discernment, and humility as we seek to know Him more.*
>
> *Thank you.*

Thanking her for her probing letter, I promised to respond thoughtfully, prayerfully, with both grace and discernment. Here's what I wrote:

> *To understand my point of view, you need to understand where I am coming from. Born and raised Jewish, I became a Christian in my mid-twenties. An evangelical Christian. I shared my testimony with Pat Robertson on the 700 Club and with Jim and Tammy Faye on the PTL Club. My articles about Christianity and the Jewish roots of the Christian faith – as well as the myriad abuses of the "prosperity preachers" and many televangelists – won awards after being published in* Christianity Today, Today's Christian Woman, Charisma, Moody Monthly, Christian

Bookstore Journal, *etc. But that was then…and this is now. After experiencing church with Roman Catholic, Episcopal, Methodist, Presbyterian, Lutheran, and Assembly of God denominations, I fellowshipped at charismatic congregations where we prayed for parking spots, claimed healing for any and all ailments, and dared not make a decision unless it was approved and sanctioned by the leadership and elders. I was exposed to a wide range of "Christian" beliefs, along with behind-the-scenes excesses and abuses that bore little resemblance to the faith Jesus preached.*

No, I don't believe that you, personally, have an agenda to further – other than judging certain behaviors of others based on what you believe the Scriptures say – but, unfortunately, when one publishes his or her beliefs in media consumed by the public, then we end up feeding "the choir" by reinforcing and adding yet more assurances that their beliefs (however misguided) are in line with the will of God. And while I certainly don't think you would approve of the words or tactics used by Fred Phelps and his Westboro Baptist Church followers, ultimately that can be what extremely happens when taking Bible verses literally and/or out of their context of time, place, and language.

I do not believe the Bible to be inerrant. I find too many discrepancies and contradictions. Any study of the history of the times and themes chronicled in the Bible shows that some things just didn't happen and others didn't happen as reported in the Bible's pages. I cannot believe that a loving and gracious God would command a chosen people to massacre and obliterate every man, woman, and child in the land in order for a master race to take root. That smacks too much of the Holocaust for me! Similarly, contrary to what's reported in the Greek Testament, there is absolutely no record or documentation whatsoever that the mass murder of young males of toddler age occurred during the reign of Herod. I could go on and on, but I won't. I simply will agree with your conclusion – which I have stated explicitly in print – that I don't believe the Bible to be inerrant or the ultimate standard.

Why not? Because I sincerely believe that God is still speaking: to us and to anyone who has ears to listen and hear.

In my humble opinion, what the Bible is depends upon who we are: For Jewish people, the Bible comprises only the Old Testament (or Covenant) and, along with a history of the chosen people and a promised land, presents rules and regulations that are impossible to follow without the need for sacrifice and blood atonement ... substituted (by rabbis) with prayer when the Temple was destroyed. For Muslims, the Judeo-Christian Bible is nothing, more or less, than background. For Christians, I believe the Bible points to the Word made flesh, the Logos: Jesus Christ. And it is this Messiah, Christ Jesus, who fulfills and reinterprets the meaning of the earlier Scriptures so wrongly enforced by the teachers of the law that it was burdensome rather than joyful to seek God's presence in our lives. Jesus, the Lord, correctly explained what the Kingdom of God is all about and paints a picture of equality, social justice, inclusion, compassion, and forgiveness. But most of all, grace ... something none of us can earn, no matter how well we memorize and recite a litany of Scriptures.

Again, I don't believe that you are hateful in speaking what you believe to be the truth. Unfortunately, too

> *many other people who lack your depth of discernment, wisdom, and love – those who read your words and simply nod – all too often have taken words they believe to be true and turned them into instruments of hatred and injustice. Need I remind you about the church's history of inquisitions, persecutions, crusades, etc. ... all, supposedly, for the "greater truth?"*
>
> *Anyway, I have digressed too much already.*
>
> *Please consider my thoughts that follow here.*
>
> *Best wishes and God bless you!*

I was enjoying our correspondence and reminded of the Scripture in Psalm 133:1, "How good and pleasant it is when God's people live together in unity!" Except, of course, that we weren't exactly there ... yet.

She replied to me:

> *We have more in common than meets the eye, because I find the internal abuses you mentioned very troubling as well. One of your (Facebook church) visuals said "Lord, save us from your followers," and that actually unearthed a thought I've had on multiple occasions. Lots of people have a problem with Jesus/the Bible primarily based on the way Christians behave. My recurring thought has been: "Does the fact that we, the believers, do not act perfectly like Christ, invalidate His message?" No. In fact, the Bible tells us that we are not perfect and that we are going to make mistakes. However, this is now being used as justification for unrighteousness, and that is quite frustrating.*

Your paper did provide a solid level of illumination for why you believe what you believe. I have recently been reading a book that has some good info on how to refute the claims of atheism/evolution. It starts with the basic premise that every person has a worldview, whether or not they realize it, and this inherently affects the way they judge evidence. I was thinking about this when reading the part on why you reject the Bible as the ultimate standard. It seems like a primary reason is that the evidence doesn't seem to match, thereby proving the biblical account inaccurate. The notion of biblical discrepancies/ contradictions is one that I heard a while ago, which has given me time to thoroughly consider the idea. This may be rather simplistic, but I feel it is a straightforward explanation for why the Bible may appear to contradict itself, or contain discrepancies. Everyone, even non-believers, acknowledge that the Bible was not written by a single person. When there are multiple authors, we should expect different perspectives, writing styles and recollections. It is analogous to 20 people witnessing the same car accident, and 20 different reports being given to the police. They are all telling the truth, but you get 20 different stories because there are 20 different perspectives.

For instance, the story of the resurrection has been called into question, but I read a very good rebuttal. The first witnesses are women. If the apostles had been in collusion, I would expect them to record men, not women, because the women lacked credibility. I would also expect all details to perfectly match among the four gospels. The fact that every word does not perfectly coincide, speaks to the authenticity. Since the core story is the same, but some of the details are not, this suggests that they didn't make it up.

This could also be the premise for many others books of the Bible. When the Bible is read as a whole, I find much compelling evidence for the claim that it is inerrant. God has made clear He can work through our weaknesses. I would assert that just because the writers were human, it does not mean that He is incapable of producing a perfect Bible through us. I suggest that the supposed lack of evidence/contradictions could also be attributed to the worldviews of the evidence-gatherers. I firmly believe they went into it with presuppositions that impacted their interpretation. Also, a lack of evidence is not the same as proving something didn't happen. I am sure there are plenty of prior events for which there is no historical proof. This singular fact is not enough to claim with certainty that "it didn't happen." Again, a person's worldview plays a major role in how they interpret the same information. We can prove this fact – just look at the way scientists can come to vastly different conclusions based on the exact same evidence. The evidence did not change, but the interpretation did since every scientist has a worldview, and they don't all believe the same thing.

The other question (how could a loving and gracious God obliterate an entire race?) is one of the most difficult to stomach. I think the question is answered when we do a full examination of His character. The Bible consistently describes Him as loving, so I take that as a given and then look at His other characteristics. He is also described as holy, righteous and just. This subsequently explains that, in addition to His love, He cannot abide sin (because He is perfect and holy). Although I am not an OT scholar, if I recall correctly, God never exacted judgment on a nation without very good reason. He loved, and at the same time, gave consequences for blatant, in-your-face sin. I would not say that those nations "got what they deserved," but rather that God had been exceedingly patient and had given them a generous amount of time to repent before destruction took place. He did not take these actions arbitrarily, and He did not want to do this. Anyone who thinks that He wants/likes/enjoys this is fundamentally misunderstanding His nature.

My mother-in-law went home to God on April 24th of this year, and she also had a tough time with the Bible passages in which God enforced punishment on rebel nations. Her thoughts were along the same lines – not being able to comprehend how a supposedly loving God could commit such atrocities. I think in light of His whole nature, rather than just a single aspect, we can gain much understanding about His actions.

I appreciate that you do not think I am being hateful, and that I have a measure of discernment, wisdom and love. I am not trying to use the Bible to divide or propagate hatred. If anyone twisted my words into hate while in my presence, you can trust that I would strongly rebuke them. In watching and reading about the happenings of the present-day church, I have been struck by the apparent deficiency of balance. What I have found is that the Grace and Truth paradox is totally balanced in Christ, but most churches seem a little "bent." They emphasize either grace or truth a little more than the other. Both extremes are not in line with Jesus' teachings, though. When there is nothing but truth, it devolves into legalism; when there is nothing but grace, it leads to moral compromise. Based on what you have written, I feel your beliefs bend toward grace. We must also speak truth though, even when it is not popular. Your desire to be 'inclusive' is wonderful, and at the same time, this must be reconciled with the exclusivity of Christianity. Jesus said He was "the Way," not "a Way" and this certainly upsets a lot of people. I would like to include everyone as well, but accepting the sacrifice of Jesus is a personal choice – it cannot be done for them, they must do it themselves. He consistently preached "Repent, for the Kingdom of Heaven is at hand!" A person must repent and die to self – you're correct that "memorizing a litany of scriptures does not earn grace." This is a love reaction after the sinner truly understands what Jesus did on their behalf – dying for their sins. A genuine believer will want to live according to His commands out of love, not duty.

God has given us rules by which to live, because they are in our best interest. Example: He says to forgive, and research indicates that bitterness (i.e. not forgiving) can make a person physically sick. His Word also directs us to meditate on His Laws, and there is published proof regarding the benefits of meditation. We should trust Jeremiah 29:11. If God defines something as sin, we should trust that He has a good reason, and live our life that way, regardless of our thoughts/feelings.

I got the distinct impression that the change in your beliefs was brought on by the sour experiences with the various churches & people you mentioned. When the leaders are being hypocrites in their own lives, people have a right to be upset. I believe that God is still speaking also, and that He can speak through His holy scriptures. If we can trust what He is speaking to us right now, why can we not also trust what He spoke to His servants in ages past?

You are right that the Bible means different things to different people. No, we do not see eye-to-eye on homosexuality, but I am OK with that. In fact, I have a friend who is bisexual. She knows my beliefs, and yet we were still able to have a civilized conversation. I am hoping that if I continue to express myself as I have with you, it will open the door to even more meaningful dialogue. If nothing else, I hope that this has offered you a compelling alternative to consider, and will draw you closer to God's truth and love, whichever direction that may be.

"The Lord bless you and keep you;

The Lord make His face shine upon you,

And be gracious to you;

The Lord lift up His countenance upon you,

And give you peace."

Numbers 6:24-26 (NKJV)

Thanks for writing.

I knew that our letters with their embedded messages were coming to an end.

Turnabout being fair play, I replied:

> *Thank you for your well thought out, beautifully articulated, and faithful response.*
>
> *There comes a point when folks have to agree to disagree ... in love.*
>
> *Can we do that?*
>
> *Experientially, theologically, and spiritually, the Lord – as our great Potter – has fashioned a "progressive" pastor out of me. As such, I push the boundaries of what was and what is in a quixotic quest to bring about what should be or could be. Your spiritual journey has been a different one, leading you to a place of trust and belief in the Bible as the full, inerrant, and authoritative Word of God. I guess, in political terminology, that would make you more of a "conservative" than me.*
>
> *Over the years, it has never ceased to astound me that churches and denominations deliberately choose to *fellowship* around their differences – focusing on what sets them apart from others – rather than on those things that "most surely are believed among us" (Luke 1:1).*
>
> *So, how about if you and I focus on those things?*
>
> *Based on our correspondence, I sincerely believe that we share more in common regarding the Lord of our lives than the points on which we differ.*
>
> *And thank you for concluding with the Aaronic benediction ... one of my favorite ways to say*

goodbye to my congregation following a worship service.

May our God bless you and nurture you and nourish you with a full measure of goodness and grace.

We worship the same God, understood differently, like children who honor their grandfather who they never met: the ones who hear their parents' stories and take them as fact; the others who conduct research on ancestry.com, finding that those stories may not be true ... but he's still grandpa.

"Everything we hear is an opinion, not a fact," stated Marcus Aurelius. "Everything we see is a perspective, not the truth."

CHRISTIAN BRANDING

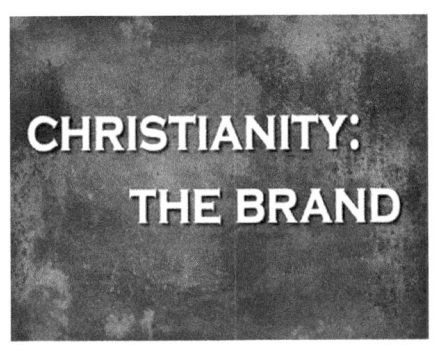

"Never has a more well-dressed, entitled, dismissive, haughty or cheap collection of Christians been seen on the face of the earth," noted Richard Beck in his "Experimental Theology" blog. Beck was talking about our tradition to follow Sunday worship services by eating out with others from our churches. The "collective behavior of the Sunday morning lunch crowd," he claimed, is the "single most damaging witness of Christianity in America today."

Beck didn't like the brand of Christianity he was seeing and wanted to know how some Christians can act humble and holy in church, yet so angry and arrogant elsewhere.

"Eleven years of my life has been dedicated to the presupposition that my greatest effectiveness was to work within the current structure of the church. The reality is, I can no longer handle the 'professionalism' of the church. I'm tired of running a nonprofit incorporation (sic) that calls itself a church," Jason Savage confessed in a Facebook post linked to his savageheartburn.com blog.

"We like our denominations, logos, productions, buildings, music, brand, staff, and social activities. We do it all in the name of ministry and talk of our kingdom advances and the souls won for Christ," he said. "But I have found that if we peel back the curtain and get past all the rhetoric … we find a crumbling church structure sighting to survive, afraid of losing our power in the community."

And, so, what brand of Christian are you?

A "brand" is used with cattle and other livestock to show ownership, whom they belong to. And so it should be with Christians: our hearts circumcised by love, as we worship and bear witness to the Lord of our lives.

Marketing experts will tell you that, for businesses, "branding" also refers to what makes your products or services so special ... and what sets them apart from the competition.

Churches also offer services ... they compete for "business" (members) ... and promote a unique, extraordinary product.

More often than not, we call that product "God."

In fact, godliness is our byproduct, evidenced by the changes we experience as we grow in grace and increasingly exhibit the fruits of the spirit sown and cultivated in communities of faith.

Churches come in all different shapes, sizes, and brands: Baptist, Episcopal, Methodist, Roman Catholic, Pentecostal, Lutheran ... the biggest and most powerful one, your corner community church, churches that speak in tongues and churches that don't ... churches that believe we'll be raptured before the great revelation and other churches that maintain Christians will be still here to suffer along with everyone else ... there are churches that worship on Saturday, the Sabbath, and those that worship on Sunday, the Lord's Day.

So, I can't help but wonder whether the God that all these churches worship is the same One as mine. Do socially conservative and socially liberal Christians actually worship the same God?

A pastor based in Seoul, Korea, posted this on Facebook:

"The typical liberal answer is 'yes' – despite our differences on issues such as homosexuality, homelessness, poverty, etc., we are united in Jesus Christ.

"It's a nice thought ... with real-life consequences which often point to the opposite being true. And one of the cornerstones of 'good theology' is that, if a theological precept doesn't ring true to real life, then it's not worth very much.

"While we may all be striving to worship the same God, it is obvious that we are not. God either relishes in his LGBTQ creation, or S/he doesn't. God either sleeps right alongside the homeless, or S/he doesn't. If God stands with the marginalized, and a self-processed, socially conservative 'Christian' does not, that person cannot be said to truly worship God—not if worship means to 'attribute worth.'"

For me, it's critically important to understand my own brand of faith and to purposefully live it, because it reinforces who I am and what I believe ... as well as attracts others to, come, follow me.

Which is something we're all called to do as disciples of Jesus, isn't it?

"Difference is part of God's creative plan for the world," says Delwin Brown in *What Does a Progressive Christian Believe?* "And if, as progressive Christians believe, God is present throughout the creation, then we must honor each form of life, each culture, each religion, with the understanding that each is a way that humans have exercised their obligation to order life, it is their way of naming their worlds. This very diversity, however, reminds us that no one viewpoint, no way of life, no culture, no religion, is perfect."

The church I currently attend calls itself, "a caring Christian community with a progressive tradition," and goes on to definite its brand by identifying some of the purposes why people come together there:

☦ To worship God;

☦ To promote personal and spiritual growth;

☦ To develop a religious community which encourages tolerance and openness of thought, and accepts diversity of thought and action;

☦ To search for meaning in life, and for understanding of ourselves through the teachings of Jesus and other great teachers;

☦ To understand how all things are related to each other, and to learn how we can best serve our local community and our world community together;

☦ To celebrate with joy the richness of ourselves and our religious community.

While the debate continues to define Progressive Christianity, a Facebook post characterized this new movement of God's Spirit: It's about "God as the dance that is the heartbeat of creation. Jesus embodying this dance. Finding our place in this dance. Moving together with God to bring healing to our world."

When I was called to pastor a church in Jacksonville, Florida, it was crucial that I understand what it believes and stands for ... to identify its brand.

"A Rainbow Spiritual Community," the sign outside the church said. That I understood. Yeah – wink, wink – I got it! We all know about rainbows and pride parades, unicorns and drag queens.

But, "Innovative Ministry in Service to God," the church's vision statement imprinted on letterhead, envelopes, business cards and brochures? What did that mean? Sounds great on paper; but what do you do with it? Especially when the words actually run contrary to practice!

We had come from a church where, at one point late in the service, we spent the first ten minutes or so sharing our joys and concerns with each other. Then, united, we wove them into our prayers of the people.

"Oh, no. You can't do that here!" I was warned when asked if I planned to make any changes in the worship service. "No, no, no, no! In this church, people will talk and talk and talk, telling you their whole life stories. They won't shut up. They'll go on and on, taking up time and you won't be able to stop them. No, no, no ... you certainly can't do that!"

Why not, I wondered? What was so wrong about learning as much as we could about the people I was charged to pastor? Why couldn't we know more about people's need(s) for prayer than what was printed in the bulletin?

I guess I should take a step back and tell you a little bit about how this church and I found each other.

Tired of the wicked Wisconsin winters and shoveling all that snow in blustery, subzero temperatures, my spouse and I came across someone who was trying to sell her house in Jacksonville.

We decided to do some research this area of Florida online.

Worshiping together has always been a foundational cornerstone of our relationship ... so, in addition to everything we Googled about Jacksonville – climate, cost of living, things to do and places to see, whether our favorite restaurants were here, what made it special – we looked for Christian churches where we could continue to worship together.

We hoped to find a progressive congregation where we could be ourselves, a place we could hug, hold hands, and praise God together with other faithful people who weren't offended by our love or thought us out of place there.

So, how do you find such a congregation? Do you type into Google, "Church – Gay – Jacksonville?" Perhaps.

But, I'll let you in on a little secret: Most churches that invite LGBT people to join them aren't so blatant ... for a variety of reasons. They don't necessarily have the word "Gay" or

"Lesbian" or the acronym "LGBT" in their online content, where search engines, like spiders, weave and report their findings.

Instead, churches like this one and others – especially until quite recently – would use "code" words that spoke to us. We knew what they meant. In days even before my time, sexual minority folks were known and introduced as "Friends of Dorothy" referred to as "festive" … people who were, "different!"

Ahhhhhhhhhhhhhh ….

And thus, over the years, when Russ and I moved around quite a bit, we came to recognize three of the primary buzz words which told people like us that the doors of a particular church were really open to us. That we'd be accepted there.

Those words?

Welcoming. Inclusive. Affirming.

I didn't really give these three words all that much thought theologically … but socially and progressively, in all good faith and fairness, they just <u>felt</u> right.

Thus began the branding of my new church and my personal spiritual journey towards the true meaning of the Gospel message and real Christianity.

Saying you're a welcoming, inclusive, and affirming congregation means more than just repeating these three words and using them as a slogan or mantra.

It means that you've got to embrace and abide in those words which name qualities of God's goodness and justice that, as Christians, we're expected to live here and now in the Kingdom of God.

Welcoming, inclusive, and affirming are vital signposts of the Way of Jesus and the way we are called to be.

Let's take a look at each of the words and see what they mean.

We'll start with "welcoming."

How many churches claim in their advertising and on their signs outside, "Everyone welcome here?" Yeah, right! Everyone welcome, except …. you, and me, and you. Fill in the blanks. It's not too hard to figure who's not really welcome and why.

Remember Sodom and Gomorrah? No, it wasn't about the sin of same-sex attraction. In fact, it wasn't about attraction at all. Quite the opposite. It was about rage and rape, about taking advantage, a lack of hospitality to others. Especially strangers. The people of Sodom and Gomorrah weren't welcoming; in fact, they were totally clueless of the angels in their midst.

> "Before they had gone to bed, all the men from every part of the city of Sodom – both young and old – surrounded the house. They called to Lot, 'Where are the men who came to you tonight?' Bring them out to us so that we can have sex with them" is how the story goes in the New International version of Genesis 19:4-5. In the Revised Standard translation, the tall tale is put this way: "But before they lay down, the men of the city, both young and old, all the people to the last man, surrounded the house; and they called to Lot, 'Where are the men you came to you tonight? Bring them out that we may know them.'"

All the men from every part of the city? The men of the city, both young and old, all the people to the last man? Even the experts – Christian and secular – don't claim that homosexual tendencies affect 100% of the male population!

This story talks about a lack of hospitality, of taking advantage of strangers.

Jesus warns of a worse judgment for those who don't show hospitality to his followers, when he dispatches them to share the

Good News: "If anyone will not welcome you or listen to your words, shake the dust off your feet when you leave that home or town. I tell you the truth, it will be more bearable for Sodom and Gomorrah on the day of judgment than for that town," he says in Matthew 10:14-15.

Welcoming churches are spiritual communities that show love and kindness, compassion, friendship and hospitality, to those that they know ... and to those that they don't. People at such churches can actually feel the touch of God's love tugging at their hearts when they greet each other, pray together, and share the peace of the Lord through word and deed.

Next on our list is "inclusive."

An inclusive church beckons all to come in and be part of their communion. Oh, I know that calling a church inclusive is a not-too-subtle euphemism, a clue that it accepts all kinds of less-than-kosher people. That's how it should be. But it also should be so much more!

Black and white, old and young, single and married, mentally handicapped and physically challenged, afflicted by all sorts of illness, demons, and distress, people who speak Spanish and English or Pig Latin, those with willing spirits but weaker flesh – whosoever! – an inclusive church should be the mortar that binds us together and to God.

Look at Jesus: Who did he hang around with? Certainly not the religious zealots presumed to be the good guys. Nope. He could be found with prostitutes and charlatans, tax collectors and publicans, a Roman centurion who loved his male servant in every sense of the word. When push came to shove, Jesus called people rejected by others to come and be with him.

For me, that's a major difference between the Old Covenant and the New:

The Hebrew Testament is exclusive; its long list of rules and regulations was designed to keep out all but a few. Those allowed in were supposed to be a nation of priests, a light to the nations. Except that they weren't. Instead, they worshiped idols and were so self-centered that they put themselves first ... even before God ... time after time.

All that changes in the New Covenant, where everyone – good and bad and in between – is invited to the wedding banquet to celebrate the blessing between Creator and creation.

"Whosoever believes." That's all it takes to be invited to feast at the tabernacle of faith and welcomed into the Kingdom of God.

But we continue to build fences, keeping people out simply because they don't believe <u>this</u> or won't accept <u>that</u>.

How silly is that ... and, oh, such a shame!

God wants us all to be one: *"Echad,"* that composite unity, like a cluster of grapes or one team with many players, the Hebrew scriptures cry out and testify, "Hear, O Israel, the Lord is our God ... the Lord alone!"

Still, we prefer to worship around our differences, the creeds and dogma and doctrines that separate us ... rather than those things that, as Luke put it, we surely believe together.

Is that so wrong, such a bad thing, to want to have a special relationship – a covenant, if you will – with certain people in given places along God's way? No, not in and of itself. But, when it excludes people from participating and treats some as better, more holy and righteous than others, then it's exclusive and contrary to God's will, I believe.

As I noted earlier: Asked which of the commandments is the greatest and most important, Jesus was quick to reply with "Love the Lord your God with all of your heart, and with all of your mind, and with all of your might." And then, in the same breath, he tacked on this addendum: "Love your neighbors as you, yourselves, would be loved." It was at that point in Luke's Gospel, Luke 10, that Jesus shares the parable of the Good

Samaritan. We've all heard it and know what it means: that even those people we don't particularly care for or would rather not be around should be treated with dignity and considered our neighbors!

Which brings me to the final word in this holy trinity of words reflecting qualities I believe God would have us be: <u>affirming</u>.

Lots of churches claim to be inclusive and welcoming. And I don't doubt their intentions. But it's one thing to invite people into your building, letting them sit in the pews. That doesn't mean, though, that the churches are supportive and positive about you, asserting and expressing their commitment to you as a beloved child of God ... just as you are.

More than recognizing that we exist and acknowledging that we're people with feelings, thoughts and, perhaps, something to contribute, affirming churches actually endorse us as made in God's image and worthy to be celebrated in who we are and what we do as God's people.

Affirming means saying "yes" rather than "no" ... looking for the positive, instead of the negative ... lifting up, not tearing down ... accepting not rejecting ... believing rather than denying or condemning ... seeking and approving the good over the bad.

After each act of creation, what did God say?

"It is good!"

It's there in the Scriptures, friends. We only need to look for it, focusing on the good news in the message instead of the bad. Remember what the Apostle Paul said about love? That it doesn't dishonor others and isn't self-serving, but rejoices with the truth. Patient and kind, love doesn't boast and isn't proud. It always protects, trusts, hopes, perseveres.

In a word, therefore, love is always affirming!

Alas, there's way too much bad theology out there, misguided Christianity that nails Jesus to the cross and crucifies him over and again, instead concentrating on the more powerful message affirmed by a risen Lord.

The world may have said "no" to Jesus when it rejected and crucified him ... but God Almighty said "yes," resurrecting him – and us! – to newness of life.

Showing hospitality comes from the heart ... it's the desire of our soul to be welcoming, loving and compassionate to others. To affirm the goodness of God and God's amazing creation.

To be inclusive is to be just and to put justice into practice. It's a matter of the mind, deciding that we're not going to show preference for one over another. God loves us all: men and women, children and elders, the healthy and the sick, the mentally challenged and the physically handicapped, heterosexuals and homosexuals, those who speak English and those who don't, white people, black people, people of every color and shade in between!

What about loving God with all of our might? Heck, that's simple:

Give somebody a helping hand. A heartfelt hug or embrace goes far to demonstrate fellowship (fillyship?) and friendship. Reaching out and shaking hands is symbolic of greeting someone and using our body language to say, "howdy!"

Even putting your hand in your pocket and reaching down deep to provide for God's Kingdom is a matter of might, of physical effort.

Each and every one of us has been created in God's image but, over the years, through socialization and worldly influences, we have lost our God-connection and ceased to act as God would have us do.

Love, compassion, and forgiveness can be abstract concepts to talk about, since we don't do enough or put into practice.

But by living welcoming, inclusive, and affirming lives, we become more loving, compassionate, and forgiving people transformed into the body of Christ and living in the Kingdom of God.

In the best of all worlds, in the Kingdom of God, love, compassion, acceptance, mercy and justice would be the rule not the exception and all churches would be faithful, fruitful communities where everyone is accepted, appreciated, and valued.

Unfortunately, human nature is such that – even in churches – it's easy to be seduced and fall into the trap of saying "Stay away!" or "Keep out!" rather than, "Come join us; we'll make room at the table for you." It's more comfortable to form cliques and circles around those we know best and longest, instead of venturing outside our comfort zone to get to know a stranger better. We find ourselves more likely to shout, "No, you can't!" than to affirm, "Yes, of course, we can!"

Welcoming. Inclusive. Affirming.

Or: Alien. Self-centered. Denying.

Which three words brand the church of Jesus Christ?

And by which of these words will you and your church be known?

WHEN OLD WINE SKINS NO LONGER FIT

DON'T GO TO CHURCH,

BE THE CHURCH.

I'm not the only one on Facebook looking for a church. A place where "religion" is more than rote and ritual. Where prayer is spontaneous and heartfelt, rather than recited from a prescribed book—whatever the edition. Where spiritual fruit, not religious nuts, is cultivated. And where the God whom I pray to is acknowledged as personifying all people ... not just a blessed, biased, and/or benevolent old man up there in the sky.

Like some of you, I'm seeking a house of worship that's truly welcoming, inclusive, and affirming—a church focused more on God's love, compassion and forgiveness than the wages of sin and a whole bunch of "thou shalt nots." I need a place where God is alive and resurrection, not crucifixion, is the focus.

Along with many people who share my faith through Facebook and the social media, I believe that it's more important for good, godly people to focus on how we live here and now ... than on whatever's awaiting in the hereafter.

So, I guess it comes down to this: I'm looking for a spiritual community that's doing church differently. One based on beliefs which don't necessarily resonate with most other churches that I know: a mustard seed growing in a place where a Christian's old wine skins may no longer be fitting.

All Christian denominations and traditions are on the threshold of change and conflict, juxtaposing what their founders and followers traditionally have held sacrosanct with what God and God's people find themselves believing today.

While there is no consensus as to a set of standard articles of faith, creeds, or accepted beliefs, I submit the following as "service marks" or starting points.

☦ **Faith is not about concrete answers, religious absolutes, creeds, or dogma.** It's about the search for understanding, the raising of important questions, the open honesty of having doubt, and the realization that no one has it all completely right; nor does any human hold all the answers. Religious absolutes of dogma, legalism, and strict doctrine can become stumbling blocks and litmus tests for who is "in" and who is "out" of the circle of God's grace. They're false tests Jesus never required that get in the way of truly believing and following the Lord's teachings.

☦ **Following Jesus is counter-cultural, radical, and disrupts the status-quo.** The good news of the Gospel is intentional in its inclusion of those who are traditionally marginalized, refused, or rejected by mainline Christianity. We all are created in the image of God and called to welcome, accept, and affirm each other.

☦ **The words of Jesus found in the Gospels – specifically, what he states are the greatest commandments: "Love God with all of your essence and love your neighbor as you should love yourself" – are to be the focus for all of his followers.** Other than that, Scripture is mostly sacred commentary that reflects the history of a particular people, the Israelites, in the Old Testament and an emerging community of Christians in the New Testament.

☦ **Recognition and affirmation of the differing belief systems of others whose faiths offer a way into relationship with God and call upon them to further God's love and grace on the**

earth is imperative. Jesus taught and revealed through example that anyone adhering to this way of life is furthering the Kingdom of God and God's message of radical love and inclusion here on earth.

✞ **Creating fellowships and communities dedicated to lifting up, affirming, and equipping one another for God's work calls us to stress being active in peace-making, striving for justice and equality of all people and nations**, loving those who are labeled by our government, society, and – at times – ourselves, as "enemies," caring for God's creation, and bringing hope to the poor and poverty-stricken, the hungry, and the hostages.

✞ **God created humans with brains capable of discovery and reason**. God does not require us to "check our brains at the door," along with our coat and hat in order to be a part of the faith. Faith and science are not in conflict; they can work together in harmony. There's nothing heretical about wrestling with God and the Bible as we struggle to find answers. After all, Jacob did!

✞ **The Church is not a four-walled institution, but a ministry without walls that surrounds and encompasses everything, everywhere**. We are all ministers whose ministry doesn't begin behind a pulpit or through spoken words; rather, our ministry is by grace that extends to all people and places ... as conveyed by our actions.

✞ **Jesus' central message is about radical inclusion**; everyone should be welcomed to participate in the congregation without judgment or forcing them to conform to our "likeness" or subscribe to any creeds in order to be accepted. We are to invite and offer <u>all</u> a place at the table – no exceptions.

In *The Heart of Christianity,* author Marcus Borg differentiates between what he refers to as the "earlier way" and the "emerging view," when examining some of the issues dividing Christians and the church today.

How does Borg's earlier way differ from the emerging view? And what is most central to Christianity and to being Christian in a time of change and conflict ... such as we're in now? The differences between the earlier and emerging ways of seeing Christianity and being Christian involve specific conflicts as well as more foundational issues: how we understand the Bible, God, Jesus, faith, and the Christian life.

Comparing Borg's earlier vs. emerging views specifically in terms of how they approach some of the issues dividing the church can be helpful:

The Bible: The earlier way maintained – and continues to – that it is the literal, inerrant, infallible Word of God, written by God to be used by mankind. The emerging belief is that the Bible introduces us to the God of the Israelite people and the founding of the Christian church. What may be real and true is not necessarily literal; mortals may have had their hands in constructing (and destructing) the Bible scriptures.

Christian exclusivism: Is there only one true religion, a single path to salvation? The earlier way of being Christian insisted that Christianity – and specific steps one had to take within Christianity – was the only way. The emerging view of Christianity believes that our Creator has been revealed to creation in different voices, different ways, different times. Reaching out to God and being accepted by God is no longer exclusive to Christianity ... especially when we understand the heart of God and the heart of Christianity.

Ordination of women: The earlier way of being Christian didn't (and still doesn't in many denominations) ordain women; the emerging way does.

Homosexuality: The earlier form of Christianity continues to regard homosexual love and behavior as sinful. You either are celibate or should seek to become heterosexual. For most of emerging Christianity, that question is already settled: What matters to God and God's people isn't <u>whom</u> you love, but <u>that</u> you love. The issues swirling around mainstream Christianity now involve the ordination of LGBT people and marriage equality for same-sex people. This debate was unimaginable only a few decades ago.

These are but a few of the issues in which different denominations and the Church universal are embroiled. For a more thorough discussion of how the earlier views and emerging values are impacting Christians in what I believe is a new "dispensation" today, I highly recommend reading Marcus Borg's *The Heart of Christianity*.

Here, however, we begin by asking ourselves: How is the Christian tradition seen? Is it about creeds and doctrines and how the Bible has, historically, been interpreted?

We also must ask: How is Christian life seen? What is it about? What is most central to it? For instance, is it about believing and doing what we need to "be saved" and have "eternal life," or is it about something else?

The earlier basis of Christianity, Borg says, is grounded in divine authority. For most Protestants, divine authority resides in the Bible—preferably the King James version; but other translations will do (up to a point). For Catholics, divine authority is believed to be in their more extensive Bible ... but also in the teaching authority of the church, expressed most clearly in the notion of papal infallibility. And in some denominations, such as the Episcopal and Anglican faith, authority is more of a three-legged stool with equal emphases on the Bible, church teachings, and traditions, along with analytic interpretation based on human experience.

The earlier form of Christianity views the Bible as a divine product: Whatever it says – no matter how seemingly contradictory or confusing – is God's truth. This includes everything from our origin and creation ... to the early history of the earth ... to how we should spend our time and talents ... to God, Jesus, ethics, and behavior. You name it: The Bible is the Word of God and God means precisely what HE said in the book!

The emerging form of Christianity doesn't claim that every jot and tittle or statement in the Bible is inerrant. Instead, it affirms that the spirit of God guided the writers from making major errors about anything that really matters to our relationship with God. Rather than assuming everything written in the Bible is meant literally, much modern Christianity believes that God can speak in parables, poetry, metaphors, and myths to make a point.

The six days of creation and Sabbath day of rest aren't necessarily 24-hour periods of time. Jonah may not have spent three days in the belly of a big fish. God may not have created different languages so that people couldn't climb the tower of Babel and become like gods. Who here knows for sure: Jesus may not actually have walked on water ... mysteriously turned water into wine ... or literally caused Lazarus to rise from the dead.

More important are the lessons about God, love, faith, and hope that these cherished tales teach us. Because it's not the letter of the law that matters most ... it's the spirit!

The emerging view of the Bible in a new dispensation of love and grace is softer and gentler. It affirms that the Spirit of God guided the writers of scripture in such a way as to prevent them from making any serious errors about anything that really matters.

What about our vision of the Christian life? How do the earlier and emerging views differ?

In the earlier basis of Christianity, faith meant belief ... and belief in everything the Bible and church taught.

The afterlife is central in the earlier Christian viewpoint. Ultimately, one should become a Christian first and foremost because of the hereafter. Wouldn't you prefer to go to heaven than hell? Moreover, the earlier emphasis of Christianity was on requirements and rewards. Do this and you'll be blessed and go to heaven; do that and you'll be damned to burn in hell.

So, one must be a good Christian! We must believe certain claims. We must confess given creeds. And we must work to sustain God's grace.

"Fear sells, until you stop buying it," one of my favorite bumper stickers says.

The earlier model believes in Christianity now for the sake of salvation later. It sees the Bible basically as God's inerrant and literal message of salvation for a blessed afterlife. And it sees the Christian life as believing what's preached from the fire-and-brimstone pulpit as the central requirement for salvation.

Let me emphasize most strongly that there is – and was – nothing intrinsically wrong with this earlier paradigm. It nourished many people and gave hope to those who suffered here and now that things would be better for them later. The Spirit of God worked through it … and continues to do so.

For now, however, I simply note that this earlier vision of Christianity has ceased to be so compelling to many in our time.

The emerging, new dispensation takes a different view.

The Bible is seen as the historical product of two former communities, ancient Israel and the early Christian movement. It wasn't written to us or for us, but for the communities that produced it. We look at the Bible and ask ourselves, "What did this mean for those communities in their historical and cultural contexts?" And then we extrapolate, contemplating, "What does this mean for us today … and overall?"

Progressive Christianity sees the Bible as sacred—not necessarily because of its origin, because "God produced it." But because, through it, the Spirit of God continues to speak to us today.

Christian life is less about rules, regulations and rewards ... and focuses, instead, on relationships and transformation.

Being Christian in this new dispensation of love and acceptance is about having a relationship – here and now – with God that transforms us and the current of our lives together. It's about making this world a better place, about making it truly a community reflecting the Kingdom of God!

Finally, the new movement of God's Spirit affirms religious pluralism. It says that, yes, you can know God and live a godly life through Judaism, Islam, Hinduism, as well as through Christianity.

Yet Christianity is distinctive and very special. It's personal and particular in terms of our response to the way we experience God. To be a Christian in this new dispensation doesn't necessarily mean believing in "Christianity," per se ... but in a special, loving relationship with God and with others.

For the progressive Christian, the message to be extracted in biblical passages must lift the content from the medium itself and be understood in terms of the person whose wisdom and way of life it points to: Christ Jesus.

Progressive Christianity is about "God as the dance that is the heartbeat of creation. Jesus embodying this dance. Finding our place in this dance. Moving together with God to bring healing to our world," as a Facebook post characterized this new movement of God's Spirit.

"Difference is part of God's creative plan for the world," says Delwin Brown in *What Does a Progressive Christian Believe?* "And if, as progressive Christians believe, God is present throughout the creation, then we must honor each form of life, each culture, each religion, with the understanding that each is a way that humans have exercised their obligation to order life, it is their way of naming their worlds. This very diversity, however, reminds us that no one viewpoint, no way of life, no culture, no religion, is perfect."

Organized religion does not have to be irrelevant, ineffectual, or repressive. Christianity can be a welcoming, intelligent, open, and collaborative approach to the life and teachings of Jesus that creates pathways into an authentic and relevant religious experience.

Ultimately, the message of the scriptures is the teachings and interpretations of a Jewish man from Galilee who lived during a time of messianic ferment when Israel suffered under Roman oppression and religious comeuppance. This, in effect, is the Gospel uttered by Jesus: a message of good news, here and now, of freedom from social debt and political bondage.

It's a message that must be understood as lived and revealed by Jesus, rather than as an extension of a medium (the "Old Covenant" or Hebrew Testament) or the "facts" and historical content hitherto taken verbatim as recounted in the oral traditions, then later transcribed into writing and transliterated from one language and culture to others.

Much Jewish law was practical, as well as spiritual. Jesus said he came not to abolish the law, but fulfill it. His sermons basically were about explaining that. We don't need to go back to Jewish law and take it literally; Jesus has given us the revised version, where he makes the relationship deeper and explains why we are to do or not do what's been proscribed in the Bible's pages.

Part of reading the Bible requires an understanding that it is contextual and historical. Israelites wandering in the desert had very strict food laws which, undoubtedly, saved many from cases of food poisoning! Later, however, Jesus said, "It is not what you put in your mouth that makes you unclean, but every evil thing that comes from the heart."

Therefore, the essential meaning of a scripture's message must be found neither in its specific words (content) nor religious tradition (medium), but rather in the person of Jesus the Christ.

Since it is through him that we have chosen to understand God's salvific purpose – to come and follow him – and call on our lives, Jesus defines and translates the message for us, because he *is* the Gospel message.

Regardless and irrespective of what exegesis is used ... which words are ascribed ... or what biblical texts are cited and conjured, it is through the lens of Jesus that God's message to us is clarified, fulfilled, and understood.

That's the good news friends; it's the *Gospel According to Facebook* and the Gospel of Jesus the Christ!

Now, consider what this means in terms of your own spiritual orientation:

• Do you find more grace in the search for meaning than in absolute certainty ... in the questions rather than in the answers?

• Do you have religious interests and yearnings, but cannot accept the dogma and doctrines you associate with Christianity?

• Still, do you find solace, meaning, and/or connection within the teachings and the path of Jesus of Nazareth?

• Do you find communion with the Sacred in the community of others seeking to live in love, with compassion and justice for all God's creation?

In the New Testament (Luke 5:10), James, John, and Simon are called "partners" (*koinonia*) whose joint participation was a shared fishing business. Koinonia was used, too, to refer to the marriage bond, while suggesting a powerful common interest that could hold two or more people together.

An incredibly rich and biblically accurate approach to building community or teamwork, Koinonia is based on a Greek word that refers to an inner goodness toward virtue and an outer goodness toward social relationships. While no single English word adequately expresses its depth and richness, Koinonia refers to a spiritual community that focuses its concerns more on meeting the needs of people than on the building, the bylaws, or annual budget.

Koinonia also relates to a spiritual relationship. The early Christian community saw this as a relationship with the Holy Spirit. The word "enthusiasm" is connected to this meaning of koinonia, as it signifies "to be imbued with the Spirit of God in us."

To create a bond of camaraderie is the meaning of koinonia when people are recognized, share their joy and pains together, and are united because of their common experiences, interests, and goals.

Fellowship creates a mutual bond, which overrides individual pride, vanity, and individualism ... fulfilling the human yearning for fraternity, belonging, and companionship.

Aiming at a common unity strives to overcome brokenness and divisiveness, ultimately gaining wholeness with each other, the environment, and our God.

Not unlike Facebook, Koinonia is a fellowship of faith focused on community, communion, and communication. Emphasizing love and compassion, the church and congregation are fully welcoming, inclusive, and affirming.

Acting out of love and compassion for others rather than selfishness and greed, Koinonia appears 19 times in most editions of the Greek New Testament. The New American Standard version of the Bible translates it as "fellowship" twelve times ... "sharing" three times ... "participation" and "contribution" (twice each).

Koinonia is integral to the *Gospel According to Facebook* and usually inspires a spiritual dimension that results in doing church differently.

DOING CHURCH DIFFERENTLY

TOWARD COMMUNITY:
UNITY IN DIVERSITY

Let me tell you about a church: It's located in one of the largest cities in the country, both in terms of geographic size and population. A coastal area with beautiful, sandy beaches and a treasure trove of history close-by, there are those who consider it "chic" and "hip," a rather cosmopolitan city, even with its small-town roots and flavor. Some say it's a special place, with its strategic seaport and major highway to other places that runs right through it.

Los Angeles, California? Long Island, New, York? Charleston, South Carolina?

Or Jacksonville, Florida, where I had been called to pastor a community church – Roman Cathoics, Methodists, Mormons, Lutherans, Presbyterians, Jews, Episcopalians, Baptists, and others familiar with the way they'd "done church" before leaving their respective churches, if not church traditions, behind – ministering, inter-denominationally, to a queer group of outcasts?

No, not quite. But we can find quite a few parallels between any of these cities and Thessalonica, one of the few New Testament cities that are still around ... as well as between the church at Thessalonia and other churches wherever.

Many churches are worthy of praise and thanksgiving to God. That's exactly what Paul was doing – celebrating the church – in his epistles to the people at the church of Thessalonia. And there are other similarities worth noting, too, between the places where we live and Thessalonia.

Thessalonia had a mixture of wealthy people, a small middle class, and then a large majority of poor people like us: slaves to the system that surrounds us.

There was tension and turmoil in Thessalonia. Rampant crime. Graffiti, obscene and objectionable words and images could be found on the walls of buildings. Murder was commonplace and divorce frequent. And, depending on whose standards were the measuring stick, morality was questionable.

Sound familiar? Uh-huh: Very much like the places where we now live!

Yet in the sea of this hedonism and crime-ridden culture was the Thessalonian church, a little island to the glory of God.

Could the same be said about your church and mine?

My time in Jacksonville had come to an end and I wondered what God would have for me next. Semi-retired and collecting Social Security, I continued teaching on the college level and serving as a "supply" pastor where and when needed ... assuming, of course, that my credentials and spiritual orientation fit the church's profile (and preferences).

Staying in touch through Facebook with people I cared about wherever they lived, we returned to our house in Virginia's Shenandoah Valley, which we had been unable to sell due to inequitable market conditions. Settling back in, we looked forward to walking down the street and rejoining Emmanuel Church. We had loved the camaraderie among the community there, always enjoyed the pastor's sermon, and appreciated the Episcopal Church's proactive stand on social justice issues that concerned us.

I thought I could pick up the pieces of my life where I'd left them four or five years earlier. But I couldn't. I no longer was the same person who had lived at that address, since my Christian beliefs and heartfelt convictions had been turned head-over-heels into entirely new directions.

The liturgy disturbed me with all of its *"Through Hims and With Hims and In Hims."* I had become acutely aware of the church's male-oriented lexicon. Why did we keep saying things like, *"O God, almighty Father, in the unity of the Holy Spirit, all glory and honor is yours, for ever and ever?"* And if the pomp and circumstance of the outfitted processional and recessional with all their glitzy glamour no longer engendered a sense of awe and holiness in me, I quickly discovered that I couldn't even mouth, silently, the words to the Nicene Creed—or any recited creed for that matter.

While Emmanuel wasn't a "high church" of smells and bells, I had laughed earlier about the curious language of the church and all its peculiar names: acolytes, albs, chancels, collects, crucifers, daily offices, fonts, fractions, litanies, propers and proper prefaces, rectors, right reverends, sacraments, sextons, vestments, vestries, vicars, and wardens.

A royal priesthood based on apostolic succession, albeit through Simon Peter now rather than Aaron, the brother of Moses?

Prayer, especially, had become a quiet and personal conversation between God and me, which couldn't be matched in time or place by any published prayers of the people or collects from the Book of Common Prayer.

"Almighty God, you have knit together your elect in one communion and fellowship in the mystical body of your Son Christ our Lord: Give us grace so to follow your blessed saints in all virtuous and godly living, that we may come to those ineffable joys that you have prepared for those who truly love you; through Jesus Christ our Lord, who with you and the Holy Spirit lives and reigns, one God, in glory everlasting. Amen."

What did these words mean to me anymore, anyway?

While I mean no disrespect and don't doubt that many of God's people can communicate and commune in such ways, this wasn't part of the Gospel I now followed. At least not according to Facebook, which played no small part in my own spiritual evolution.

I had been exposed to the church's dirty laundry and experienced its power plays firsthand, including the stigma of social strata among the very desirables, desirables, and less-than-desirables within too many churches.

Convinced that the church was complicit – if not a primary culprit – in belittling women, I cringed every time "He" replaced God as a pronoun repeatedly throughout the service.

Rewards and retribution, heaven or hell in the hereafter, weren't what going to church was about, anymore, nor was it a "must-do" on my calendar for fear of the guilt in displeasing God.

Passing the peace, like passing the plate, had become no more or less than going through the motions … and the routine, predictable liturgies weren't satisfying anymore. I felt spiritually malnourished. The top-down, classroom approach to worship where everyone faced front silently, looking and listening to the pastor or preacher (except when designated to respond as indicated) chaffed at my spirit, which longed to participate, wanting to soar.

The anatomy of a worship service I envisioned was much more informal: People come together, first, to eat and socialize. Then, as the service is about to start, all sit down at tables, not pews, with their food and beverages. Didn't Jesus do much of his teaching over meals with others? Greetings and announcements are offered. Uplifting songs sung. Scriptures read. A pastor-moderator then shares some thoughts and ideas about possible meanings of the biblical text back when it was written … as well as its potential relevance to us in our lives here today. A short discussion – conversation – continues the narrative, leading to the sharing of our personal joys and concerns. Knowing what's on our minds and in our hearts, together we pray. Sharing the sacrament of communion, we're invited to abide in the Lord and celebrate God abiding in us. Worship concludes with a song of praise or thanksgiving, as we leave, encouraging each other to "go in peace to serve the Lord."

Surely, in a community of nearly 25,000 people boasting scores of churches, there had to be at least one to which God would be calling me.

There wasn't. Not a single one ... at least not within a 30-minute commute. Believing that church should be part and parcel of my community to fulfill its mission to the poor, the homeless, the hungry, the destitute, I nevertheless ventured away from my home turf to see what was out there. But, no matter how far I moved from my community, as with Jonah, God kept calling me back.

"Maybe God's calling you to start a church, a new church, like the one you've been talking about?" proposed some who knew me and had been following my Facebook posts about God's grace, love, compassion, and forgiveness.

Still a neophyte and nascent pastor, what did I know about planting churches? Nonetheless, I couldn't help but believe that other kindred spirits were on the same sacred path, seeking more than what already existed in our churches.

So, announcing a new spiritual community forming, I turned to Facebook and created a "page" – where businesses, organizations and brands can share their stories and connect with people – about Shalom Spiritual Community, a new church being started. I began by describing our mission:

Like many of our brothers and sisters in Christ, we echo these core practices as goals and objectives of what we value ... and will commit ourselves to do our best by living them out collectively, as individuals and as a community:

- ***Inviting****: We invite <u>all</u> to experience God's grace through the Gospel and to become engaged in the Kingdom of God with us.*

- ***Welcoming****: We want to provide a safe and welcoming space so that every individual is comfortable expressing concerns, celebrations, doubts, fears, and questions. We encourage and support you to be the person you were created to be in God's image.*

- ***Journeying****: We see ourselves as mutual travelers seeking to follow Christ in the midst of our daily lives. We acknowledge that none of us has arrived yet ... we have much to learn ... and that, for us, church is a journey ... not destination.*

- ***Affirming****: We believe that too much emphasis is placed on the crucified Jesus and not enough on the resurrected Lord of our lives. Rather than be strict law-enforcers focused on rewards and punishments, we seek to be grace-givers recognizing the goodness of God, God's works, God's people, and God's creation.*

- ***Connecting****: We recognize that it is through relationships that we experience communion: connection with God and with one another. We come together in larger and smaller groups or partnerships to encourage, challenge, worship, discuss, and discover the ways God is calling us to live.*

- ***Collaborating****: We strive to be responsible, serving our neighbors in need and committed to collaborating with other community groups and organizations in fulfilling this part of our mission.*

- ***Re-imagining and Re-purposing****: We respect our rich Judeo-Christian heritage, but also value our freedom to creatively re-imagine the church in our current context. We are committed to questioning and critiquing our existing practices, and are open to God's guidance into new expressions of church.*

Lo and behold, people *liked* my posts and shared them with others, adding comments that appeared to indicate their support for our new church.

By the time we reached about 50 people engaged in our spiritual community's communications, I decided it was time to get together in "real-time" and hold our first worship service in the living room of our home.

About a dozen or so people showed up, including an ordained United Church of Christ minister who worked as a chaplain in a nearby assisted living facility. She brought a handicapped patient in a wheelchair with her. A recently married, middle-aged couple who worked with me at the area college came; the husband, a musician, sat at my 1905 Haines upright piano and led us in song. Also attending was a newly-widowed woman who actively participated in our conversations online. There were two gay couples, male and female, and two of our neighbors who lived on the same block. A Latino man was glad to find fellowship among others who accepted him, even if I was the only one fluent in his native language. My partner and I, of course, were there to host the gathering.

Our time together passed quickly and everyone seemed quite comfortable with the service. We talked and prayed and sang and shared communion, until it was time to figure out where and when we'd next meet. Pulling out their digital devices and pocket calendars, we decided to get together a month later—same time, same place.

When the day arrived, however, there only were eight of us. The chaplain's schedule had been changed, requiring her to work on Sundays; one of our couples were away for the weekend; and the newlyweds confided that they felt guilty about abandoning their Presbyterian church after signing up to serve in leadership positions with its altar guild and music ministry.

Those of us there truly were blessed by our worship ... but something was missing: people. Sure, more than two of us had gathered in the Lord's name, but a sense of community was lacking with just eight. It didn't get any easier. We just couldn't coordinate our busy and conflicting schedules to appoint specific times to meet. And so it went ...

Meanwhile, ironically, our Shalom Spiritual Community on Facebook was growing by leaps and bounds. Every day, I'd post a new meditation, which people apparently liked and shared. New people became engaged, actively following our posts and responding to them accordingly. A number of people asked for prayer, which we provided—collectively and individually. Several sought my advice and pastoral counseling through *private messages* or over the phone ... and, once or twice, using Skype.

God's love was poured out and shed abroad in our hearts through the Holy Spirit, which had been given to us. We were becoming a koinonia community, even if on Facebook.

Plenty of churches have had a Facebook presence, usually as an adjunct to their own websites. For these churches, Facebook and other social media facilitate news spreading more efficiently among members and provide a networking option for sharing sermon links and graphic communications.

For us, however, Facebook was becoming a more dynamic meeting place, regularly drawing in the community to share glad tidings, gossip, special needs, and prayer requests. The church had extended its tent and borders beyond the building and a single day – Sunday – to become a place where people engaged and interacted more or less daily.

Our "congregation" was different from others, as well: We were attracting people who considered themselves Christians but couldn't, or wouldn't, attend their local churches. Some had suffered hurtful experiences there, while others liked Christ's message but not the Christians who followed him. A number in our community were handicapped or lacked transportation, so gathering online with us was their spiritual lifeline. Most, however, continued to attend church where they lived for a variety of reasons – family, neighbors, tradition, guilt – but wanted something more, something different, than they were getting in their pews. They felt spiritually malnourished. Undoubtedly, some also liked the fact that we weren't asking for money.

"How do you pass the plate?" was among their first questions. "Am I expected to give or tithe?" "Where does the money come from?" "How is it being used?"

That's part of the beauty of this ministry.

As a (semi-retired) pastor still working part-time as a college professor – and collecting Social Security – I didn't expect to be supported financially. And, since we have neither building nor facilities and staff to support, funding isn't needed there either. Maybe we expect too much of the "hired hands" – pastor, music director, administrators and clerks, cleaning crews, etc. – we employ at our churches? God has endowed us with many gifts and talents! Could it be that we should be taking more responsibility for getting involved and personally participating?

"Cheap church" declared some of our doubters and detractors. Maybe so. But would Jesus judge a church on the merits of its revenue stream?

More importantly, especially as it concerns the *Gospel According to Facebook,* is what did Jesus mean when he referred to his <u>church</u> in Matthew 16:18?

☦ "And I tell you that you are Peter, and on this rock I will build my church, and the gates of Hades will not overcome it." (New International Version)

☦ "Now I say to you that you are Peter (which means 'rock'), and upon this rock I will build my church, and all the powers of hell will not conquer it." (New Living Translation)

Was Jesus literally talking about a rock (as in bricks and stones and mortar used to erect buildings)? Or was he talking metaphorically, about an enduring faith focused on living in the Kingdom of God here, now, and eternally?

Seriously, I doubt Jesus would ever have imagined the church buildings and cathedrals along with their priceless artwork and artifacts that people have come to worship as well as – and apart from – the Lord. I suspect that Jesus' idea of "church" and "ministry" is quite different than ours.

Rather than telling us to be concerned about the utility bills and staff benefits and church maintenance costs, Jesus was quite specific about where and how our treasures were to be used: to help others.

Honestly, I do believe it is our responsibility to give back to God and support the needs of God's creation. So, whatever their preferred charity – the American Red Cross Disaster Fund ... a local homeless shelter, food pantry, or soup kitchen ... the American Humane Society ... World Vision ... whatever – we ask our people to be faithful in their giving—whether of their time and/or financial resources.

"We'd be honored if you gave to your favorite nonprofit organization as a tribute to Shalom Spiritual Community," we repeatedly stated on Facebook. "Just be careful to check the charity out and make sure that it's inclusive and doesn't deny God's unconditional, uncompromising love to anyone."

Picking up again on the parallels I cited at the beginning of this chapter between our brave new world church and the church at Thessalonia, perhaps the most critical and striking one for me in terms of similarities is that the Thessalonian church was a new and different kind of church, made up of new and different people. Just as Thessalonia was the first church whose congregation, essentially, were non-Jewish people, our Shalom Spiritual Community is among the first progressive churches to reside on Facebook and become populated by fair-minded, open-hearted people.

Within two years, our average daily "attendance" exceeded hundreds of people who viewed, liked, shared, and/or commented on our messages.

Along with daily devotionals and short meditations (which seem to work best on Facebook), we stream music for those wanting a choir ... post links to blogs for those seeking more in-depth sermons and spiritual studies ... YouTube videos virtually provide a different tempo and tone for special messages. And, while we have yet to share sacraments like communion – which, one of these days, we hope to somehow incorporate – we continue to relate, pray for one another, share our joys and concerns together, and fulfill the Kingdom of God.

As this book is being produced, here's what we know about those currently engaged in the Shalom Spiritual Community:

• We have well over 400 *members* (people who like and regularly participate in the posts on our page). While we gain about ten new members each month, we lose one or two. Most people involved with our church ministry have been referred to us by others.

• In any given week, our reach – representing the total number of people who have been exposed to our posts – comprises well over 2,000 people ... who, because of our members, have seen and reacted to our messages. By sharing the "good news," some would consider us evangelical.

• On average, each of our posts is seen by about 370 people.

• While our membership varies, at most times we comprise about 53% men and 47% women. A breakdown by age of our online spiritual community shows that 27% are between 45-54; 25% are between 35-44; 24% are between 55-64; 10% are between 25-

34; 10% are >65; and 7% are between 18-24. Ironically (for the Internet), we're more middle-aged than young or old.

• Although we are reaching people in more than 50 countries, more of our most actively engaged live in the United States, United Kingdom, Australia, India, Mexico, Canada, Netherlands, Singapore, Philippines, and Liberia.

• People reached, for the most part, live in the USA, Australia, New Zealand, United Kingdom, Canada, India, Philippines, Panama, Mexico, and Spain.

• The top ten US cities where our *members* live are those in which I (the pastor) have lived and/or had some personal contact: Staunton, VA; Jacksonville, FL; Racine, WI; Milwaukee, WI; Sturgeon Bay, WI; Kenosha, WI; Washington, DC; Waynesboro, VA; Roanoke, VA; and Birmingham, AL.

• The top ten cities receiving our messages, however, vary considerably: Sydney, NW, Australia; Christchurch/Canterbury, New Zealand; Kenosha, WI; Racine, WI; Racine, WI; Jacksonville, FL; Milwaukee, WI; Dunedin, New Zealand; Manchester, England; Chicago, IL; and Staunton, VA.

• Languages spoken by those who spend the most time with us predominantly are English (US and UK) along with Spanish, Danish, Indonesian, Japanese, and German. What's more, we reach people who speak French, Vietnamese, Greek, and Polish, among other languages.

Much like the church at Thessalonia, Shalom Spiritual Community is a place where God is honored and praised.

We're certainly not perfect. Far from it! And we're not even the best there is. But we are blessed of God, and the Spirit of God surely has been present with us in this remarkable (URL) location.

The Apostle Paul spends time affirming those in the church of Thessalonia. In verses 2-3 of 1 Thessalonians (NAS), he writes,

"We give thanks to God always for all of you, making mention of you in our prayers, constantly bearing in mind the work of faith and labor of love and steadfastness of hope in our Lord Jesus Christ in the presence of our God and Father."

Three little words – <u>faith</u>, <u>hope</u>, and <u>love</u> –jump out at me, recalling that beautiful passage so many people are fond of from I Corinthians 13: "And now these three remain: faith, hope, and love. But the greatest of these is love."

Despite their differences – they're mostly Gentiles rather than Jews – Paul is confident that the Thessalonians are loved and accepted by God, just as I am certain that the same can be said of Shalom Spiritual Community.

Whosoever believes – whosoever! –is loved by the Lord God … and that's the way it should be at every church, everywhere.

Like the church at Thessalonia, our online community isn't really typical of many churches today. Nevertheless, I believe that both churches represent God's ideal—the type of church God wants every church to become: wonderful places to be, to share, and to worship.

The Thessalonians became a living example to other believers, we're told in verse 7. In other words, it's not enough to just live our lives among other Christians in isolation.

We're called to more directly use and channel our influence with others.

Too many people have turned away – or <u>been</u> turned away – from the church and, in the process, find themselves turned off to the God that created them and continues to love them unconditionally.

Hurt, bigotry, judgment, condemnation and rejection from much of the religious establishment indeed are what have brought many people to Shalom Spiritual Community.

It's now up to us to share the good news, sensitively and sensibly, with others. We're called to speak with full conviction, aware that God has given us a very special mission field to which few are called and even fewer yet choose to go.

People saw a change in those who worshipped at Thessalonia. They had become better people – more loving, compassionate, giving, and thankful – because of their faith and their beliefs.

We all know what happens when people are branded as being different: they're talked about ... and lots of people talked up the church at Thessalonia, telling others about the amazing things that were happening there.

Modern PR people call this word-of-mouth marketing ... and it's the best advertising there is. On Facebook, it's simply called "sharing."

The history of the Thessalonian church is a story about what can happen when everything goes right, the way God wants it to be: Paul and his team quickly planted a vibrant and healthy church that reached out to others, touching and turning many lives around for the better.

My own prayer is that *The Gospel According to Facebook* and virtual churches like Shalom Spiritual Community will continue to share a message attracting people to places they want to be because God is there, helping and healing and loving and blessing and making us faithful communities worthy of praise.

Social Media and the Good News

PREFACE

Jesus doesn't care how Many bible verses you have memorized.

He cares about how you treat people.

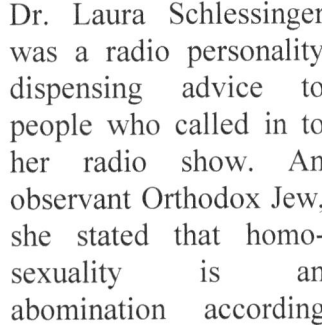

Dr. Laura Schlessinger was a radio personality dispensing advice to people who called in to her radio show. An observant Orthodox Jew, she stated that homosexuality is an abomination according to Leviticus 18:22 and cannot be condoned under any circumstance. Not long after making these comments, an open letter to her, "Why Can't I Own a Canadian?" went viral on the Internet.

Dear Dr. Laura:

Thank you for doing so much to educate people regarding God's Law. I have learned a great deal from your show, and try to share that knowledge with as many people as I can. When someone tries to defend the homosexual lifestyle, for example, I simply remind them that Leviticus 18:22 clearly states it to be an abomination. End of debate. I do need some advice from you, however, regarding some of the other specific laws and how to follow them:

When I burn a bull on the altar as a sacrifice, I know it creates a pleasing odor for the Lord - Lev.1:9. The problem is my neighbors. They claim the odor is not pleasing to them. Should I smite them?

I would like to sell my daughter into slavery, as sanctioned in Exodus 21:7. In this day and age, what do you think would be a fair price for her?

I know that I am allowed no contact with a woman while she is in her period of menstrual uncleanliness - Lev.15:19- 24. The problem is, how do I tell? I have tried asking, but most women take offense.

Lev. 25:44 states that I may indeed possess slaves, both male and female, provided they are purchased from neighboring nations. A friend of mine claims that this applies to Mexicans, but not Canadians. Can you clarify? Why can't I own Canadians?

I have a neighbor who insists on working on the Sabbath. Exodus 35:2 clearly states he should be put to death. Am I morally obligated to kill him myself?

A friend of mine feels that even though eating shellfish is an abomination - Lev. 11:10, it is a lesser abomination than homosexuality. I don't agree. Can you settle this?

Lev. 21:20 states that I may not approach the altar of God if I have a defect in my sight. I have to admit that I wear reading glasses. Does my vision have to be 20/20, or is there some wiggle room here?

Most of my male friends get their hair trimmed, including the hair around their temples, even though this is expressly forbidden by Lev. 19:27. How should they die?

I know from Lev. 11:6-8 that touching the skin of a dead pig makes me unclean, but may I still play football if I wear gloves?

My uncle has a farm. He violates Lev. 19:19 by planting two different crops in the same field, as does his wife by wearing garments made of two different kinds of thread (cotton/polyester blend). He also tends to curse and blaspheme a lot. Is it really necessary that we go to all the trouble of getting the whole town together to stone them? - Lev.24:10-16. Couldn't we just burn them to death at a private family affair like we do with people who sleep with their in-laws? (Lev. 20:14)

I know you have studied these things extensively, so I am confident you can help. Thank you again for reminding us that God's word is eternal and unchanging.

Your devoted fan,

Jim

Many Christians and Jewish people do understand that truth and reality in the Bible doesn't mean that everything in its pages is necessarily factual.

"Here at Christians Tired of Being Misrepresented, we take the Bible seriously, but not literally," posted this Facebook group, asking those who wish to take the Bible literally to take the following two scriptures literally, too.

• Ezekiel 16:49-50: "The sin of your sister Sodom was this: She lived with her daughters in the lap of luxury - proud, gluttonous, and lazy. They ignored the oppressed and the poor. They put on airs and lived obscene lives. And you know what happened: I did away with them."

• Leviticus 19:27: "Don't cut the hair on the sides of your head or trim your beard."

Believing that the Bible is replete with other examples of verbiage not meant to be taken quite literally, the group asked for other examples of scriptures that don't quite make sense or add up anymore.

Contributions included these …

Exodus 21:7: "If a man sells his daughter as a servant, she is not to go free as male servants do."

Deuteronomy 21:10-14: "When you go out to war against your enemies, and the Lord your God delivers them into your hand, and you take them captive, and you see among the captives a beautiful woman, and desire her and would take her for your wife, then you shall bring her home to your house, and she shall shave her head and trim her nails. She shall put off the clothes of her captivity, remain in your house, and mourn her father and her mother a full month; after that you may go in to her and be her husband, and she shall be your wife. And it shall be, if you have no delight in her, then you shall set her free, but you certainly shall not sell her for money; you shall not treat her brutally, because you have humbled her."

Deuteronomy 21: 18-21: "If someone has a stubborn and rebellious son who will not obey his father and mother, who does not heed them when they discipline him, then his father and his mother shall take hold of him and bring him out to the elders of his town at the gate of that place. They shall say to the elders of his town, 'This son of ours is stubborn and rebellious. He will not obey us. He is a glutton and a drunkard.' Then all the men of the town shall stone him to death. So you shall purge the evil from your midst; and all Israel will hear, and be afraid."

Deuteronomy 22:28–29: "If a man meets a virgin who is not betrothed, and seizes her and lies with her, and they are found, then the man who lay with her shall give to the father of the young woman fifty shekels of silver, and she shall be his wife, because he has violated her. He may not divorce her all his days."

Deuteronomy 23:1: "If a man is crushed, wounded or cut in his male member, he shall not enter the assembly of the Lord."

Deuteronomy 23:2: "No bastard shall enter the Lord's assembly, even unto the tenth generation none of his descendants shall ever go into the assembly of the Lord."

Deuteronomy 25:11: "When two men are fighting and the wife of one of them intervenes to drag her husband clear of his opponent, if she puts out her hand and catches hold of the man by his privates, you must cut off her hand and show her no mercy."

Song of Solomon 8:8: "We have a little sister and she has no breasts. What will we do for our sister on the day when she is spoken for?"

1 Corinthians 7:1: "Concerning what you had written about, it is not good for a man to marry."

1 Corinthians 11:7: "Does not the very nature of things teach you that if a man has long hair, it is a disgrace to him?"

1 Corinthians 14:33-34: "As in all the churches of the saints, the women should keep silent in the churches. For they are not permitted to speak, but should be in submission, as the Law also says. If there is anything they desire to learn, let them ask their husbands at home. For it is shameful for a woman to speak in church."

Galatians 3:28: "There is neither Jew nor Gentile, neither slave nor free, nor is there male and female, for you are all one in Christ Jesus."

I Peter 2:18: "Slaves, in reverent fear of God submit yourselves to your masters, not only to those who are good and considerate, but also to those who are harsh."

"Heck, you could make a pretty good biblical case for gluttony being a lifestyle since that has been normalized by our culture of 'Supersized' portions and overflowing buffet lines, charged author Rachel Held Evans in her blog posted on Facebook, "starting with passages like Philippians 3:19 (their god is their belly), Psalm 78: 18 (they tested God in their heart by demanding the food they craved), Proverbs 23:20 (be not among drunkards or among gluttonous eaters of meat), Proverbs 23:2 (put a knife to your throat if you are given to appetite), or better yet, Ezekiel 16:49 (Now this was the sin of your sister Sodom: She and her daughters were arrogant, overfed and unconcerned; they did not help the poor and needy.)."

Even for the Christmas season, an interesting passage is Jeremiah 10:3: "For the customs of the peoples are worthless; they cut a tree out of the forest, and a craftsman shapes it with his chisel. They adorn it with silver and gold; they fasten it with hammer and nails so it will not totter."

A pastor once told me, "The Bible is much too important to take literally."

"The effort to untangle the human words from the divine seems not only futile to me but also unnecessary, since God works with what is, believes Barbara Brown Taylor. In *Leaving Church* she says, "God uses whatever is usable in life, both to speak and act, and those who insist on fireworks in the sky may miss the electricity that sparks the human heart."

Does it really matter to me if God created everything in six days and rested on the seventh? Or that two of every species were aboard an ark to save them from flooding and annihilation? Maybe Moses didn't personally part the Red Sea and Mary, mother of Jesus, might have been just a young girl if not a virgin? And – perish the thought! – what if Jesus' human body wasn't actually raised from the dead? In the end, does it really, really matter?

Details. After all, they're just details! And here's a case where the old adage "the devil is in the details" may <u>literally</u> be true.

I might not believe everything stated in the Bible as empirical and factual, but faith wants my mind to be at peace. No matter what I can or cannot accept at face value, my faith, hope, and love are ultimately bigger than that, because I believe in the blessed God who emerges.

More essential to me is that, two thousand years after he walked and taught, healed and released his followers from all sorts of bondage, the body of Christ continues to grow. It now numbers more than two billion souls, greater than 30% of the world's population.

It all comes down to faith and belief.

Remember Dante's *Divine Comedy?* During his journey with Virgil through the three realms of the dead – *Inferno, Purgatorio,* and *Paradiso* – Dante is able to use his mind to reason his way through each of the concentric circles leading out of hell. But logic doesn't help him to escape to the next realm. No, that requires a quantum leap of faith.

Along with Christians Tired of Being Misrepresented, quite a few Facebook groups have been created to urge more tolerance and less literalism than the church institutional has been known to practice. Among them: Unfundamentalist Christians, Christians for a Change, Rethink Church, Progressive Christian Alliance, The Christian Left, Trying God's Patience, and Kissing Fish: Christianity for People Who Don't Like Christianity.

The issue for groups like these isn't whether a verse or anecdote in the Bible is true, but what the truth in that story – the pearl of great value – is for us.

"The Bible may have been divinely inspired, but it's got human fingerprints all over it," one Facebook fan maintained.

"It's a wonderful book written in rich and varied literary forms," another stated, "but poetry is poetry; allegory is allegory; etc. How rich is God's word!"

Many believe in Bible as sacred history and literature, wonderful stories. Truth is in there ... by what it means, not always what it says. This best-selling book of all time tells of the experiences recounted by the first monotheists, the Hebrews, in the "Old" Testament (or Covenant), and the emerging Christian community in the "New."

Facebook followers might not be able to tell you precisely what they believe (or don't) based on established criteria; they cannot codify their beliefs into a creed or statement of faith.

Yet they have faith in God, a greater good, a higher power.

Diana Butler Bass, in her book *Christianity after Religion: The End of the Church and the Birth of a New Spiritual Awakening*, discusses the changing face of religion in America. In one section of the book, Dr. Bass talks about an exercise she would do as she went from church to church and from denominational meeting to denominational meeting to present her material. She would ask the people at these events to do a word association exercise in which they would list all the words that they associate with "religion" vs. the words they associate with "spirituality." No matter where she was – regardless of denomination – she found surprisingly similar results.

Religion was always associated with words such as "structure," "rules," "building," "order," and "authority": rigid, inactive, strong but lifeless words.

Spirituality, however, brought to mind words like "experience," "connection," "transcendence," and "energy." These words have a sense of life to them, of being open to change and dynamic.

Some congregations were skeptical of the word "spirituality," Dr. Bass wrote, and would describe it with a few more negative terms. Even so, she remarked, "religion got the worst of it:

'cold,' 'outdated,' 'rigid,' 'hurtful,' 'narrow,' 'controlling,' 'embarrassing,' and 'mean.' No matter the religion or denomination, all of the groups associated spirituality with experience ... and religion with institutions."

So it seems that spirituality is more apt to capture the sense of Christianity that we're about in our own online congregation.

"Religion is for people afraid of going to hell. Spirituality is for people who already have been there," one Facebook post appeared to joke. Another post, attributed to *Inside the Divine Pattern* by Anthony Dogulas Williams, put it like this: "Religion comes from doctrines and words. Spirituality comes from our hearts and souls."

People who follow the *Gospel According to Facebook* tend to be spiritual, if not religious, more open-minded than closed. They worship God, not the Bible, and believe that there are many ways to encounter the Sacred ... even though their faith tells them that Jesus got it right and is showing us the way.

These are people who look directly to the Christ – to Jesus – through the inspiration of the Holy Spirit for answers to their questions, rather than to doctrines or dogma of the religious establishment. That's why they're also interested in the words of the Buddha, Desmond Tutu, Dalai Lama, Gandhi, and others who speak divine truisms.

We're people preferring actions over words, inclusion over exclusion, love above all else. Compassion and forgiveness supersede judgment. How we live and treat one another here and now takes precedence over the hereafter. Believing that the Kingdom of God can be here among us, ours is a Facebook community that respects humility in religious observances rather than mega-church galas and self-aggrandizement.

Grace and love go hand-in-hand; both are gifts to be cherished and cultivated: talked, walked, and shared.

For us, "church" is people, not a building or institution.

If you, too, agree with this vision, then you will probably relate to the proverbs and words of wisdom collected from Facebook, Twitter, and other social media on the following pages.

Contemplate them, meditate on them, and consider using them as your daily devotionals.

Shalom.

Part Two ...

Collected Wisdom and Proverbs

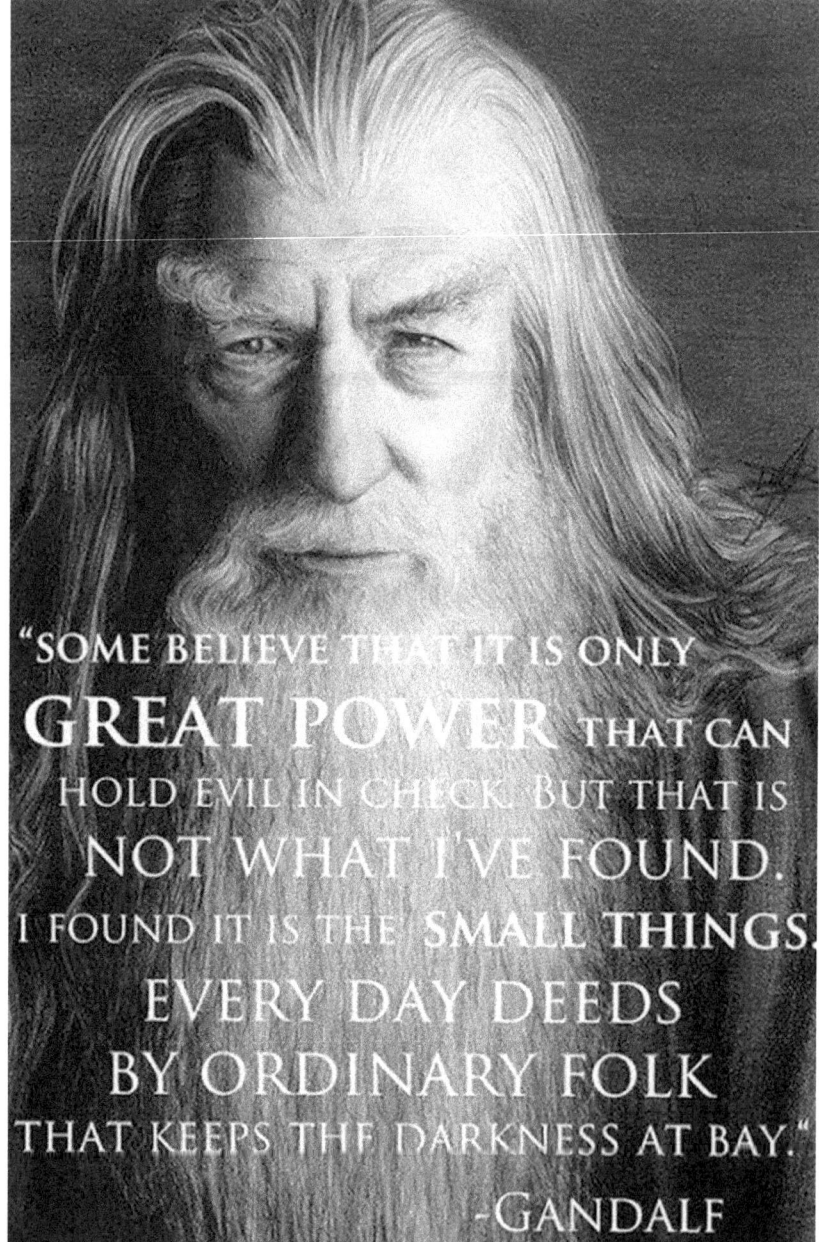

Grace isn't a little prayer
you say before receiving a meal.

It's a way to live.

"For it is in giving that we receive."

–St. Francis of Assisi

"You can judge the character of a man by how he treats those who can do nothing for him."

–James D. Miles

Someone else is praying for the things you take for granted.

Speak in such a way that others love to listen to you. Listen in such a way that others love to speak to you.

Life is a series of thousands of tiny miracles.
Notice them.

"Life is speaking to you. You may not always like what it is saying, but you still have to listen."

–Sheila Burke,
Chorus of Souls

"Sure sign of spiritual growth: You want more freedom and less stuff."

–Lisa Villa Prosen,
My Renewed Mind

Give birth to something ... a solution, a creation, an idea, a dream. The pulse of life will surge through you.

A tongue has no bones but it is strong enough to break a heart.

Be careful with your words.

"Any prejudice, whether it is based on race, ethnicity, gender, sexual orientation, cult or ritual purity, is finally nothing but a dagger aimed at the very heart of this gospel that arises from Jesus' life."

–Bishop John Shelby Spong

I am no longer accepting the things I cannot change. I am changing the things I cannot accept.

"Blessed are the peacemakers. For they shall be called the children of God."

–Matthew 5:9

If we coud look into the hearts of others and understand the hardships that every one of us faces daily, I think that we would treat each other with more gentleness, patience, tolerance and care.

"You will have to find what sparks a light in you so that you, in your own way, can illuminate the world."

–Oprah Winfrey

Be a witness, not a judge.

Focus on yourself, not on others.

Listen to your heart, not to the crowd.

"Religion comes from doctrines and words. Spirituality comes from our hearts and souls."

–Anthony Douglas Williams,
Inside the Divine Pattern

"Our souls make us spiritual beings. Our bodies make us human beings."

-Anthony Douglas Williams,
Inside the Divine Pattern

"Rules to live by: Express gratitude. Keep your promises. Say, 'I love you.' Be gentle with others. Speak the truth. Share your love. Laugh at yourself. Use words of kindness. Consider others. Do your best."

–Fiona Childs

"A man who conquers himself is greater than one who conquers a thousand men in battle."

–Buddha

"You are never too old to set another goal or to dream a new dream."

–C.S. Lewis

If you're lucky enough to be different, don't ever change.

"Sometimes, the smallest step in the right direction ends up being the biggest step of your life. Tip toe if you must, but take that step."

–GemmaStone.org

"I'm proud of the scars in my soul. They remind me that I have an intense life."

–Paulo Coelho

Never forget the three powerful resources you always have available to you: love, prayer, and forgiveness.

"There comes a point where you have to realize that you'll never be good enough for some people. The question is, is that your problem or theirs?"

–Life Is a Beautiful Struggle

"I cannot do all the good the world needs, but the world needs all the good I can do."

–Jana Stanfield

Sometimes, God calms the storm ... sometimes God lets the storm rage and calms His children.

Do not conform.

Let God transform you.

"I sought to hear the voice of God and climbed the topmost steeple, but God declared:

'Go down again—I dwell among the people.'"

–John Henry Newman

"The most powerful weapon on earth is the human soul on fire."

–Ferdinand Foch

Be kind to unkind people.

They need it most.

"I do not at all understand the mystery of grace—
only that it meets us where we are but does not
leave us where it found us."

–Anne Lamott

"I do not feel obligated to believe that the same God who has endowed us with senses, reason, and intellect has intended us to forgo their use and by some other means to give us knowledge which we can attain by them."

–Galileo Calilel

The life you live is the lesson you teach.

Our job is to love others without stopping to inquire whether or not they are worthy.

"Not all those who wander are lost."

–J.R.R. Tolkien

"Most people do not see their beliefs.

Instead, their beliefs tell them what they see.

This is the simple difference between clarity and confusion."

–Matt Kahn

One tree can start a forest.
One smile can begin a friendship.
One hand can lift a soul.
One word can frame the goal.
One candle can wipe out darkness.
One laugh can conquer gloom.
One hope can raise your spirits.
One touch can show you care.
One life can make the difference.
Be that one today.

"To be yourself in a world that is constantly trying to make you something else is the greatest accomplishment."

–Ralph Waldo Emerson

I'd rather have a mind opened by wonder than one closed by belief.

To be kind is more important than to be right.

Many times, what people need is not a brilliant mind that speaks, but a special heart that listens.

Follow God, not people.

Love the people God gave you, because God will need them back one day.

"There are hundreds of paths up the mountain, all leading to the same place.

So it doesn't matter which path you take.

The only person wasting time is the one who runs around the mountain telling everyone that his or her path is wrong."

–Hindu proverb

I'm not where I need to be; but, thank God, I'm not where I used to be.

Every day you hear people saying what they want.

Well, this is what I want:

I want people who are sick to be healed. I want children with no families to be adopted. I want people never to have to worry about food and shelter and heat.

Most of all, I want to see people start to care for one another.

Don't believe everything you hear from some "Christians."

I love you ... no matter what!

–God

"Difference is of the essence of humanity. Difference is an accident of birth and it should, therefore, never be the source of hatred or conflict. The answer to difference is to respect it. Therein lies a most fundamental principle of peace: respect for diversity."

–John Hume

"What lies behind us and what lies before us are small matters compared to what lies within us."

–Ralph Waldo Emerson

"If you truly loved yourself, you could never hurt another."

–Buddha

If you stumble, make it part of the dance.

Imagine with all your mind.

Believe with all your heart.

Achieve with all your might.

You laugh at me because I'm different.

I laugh at you because you're all the same.

Whenever you don't understand what's happening in your life, just close your eyes … take a deep breath and say:

"God, I know it is your plan. Please, just help me through it."

In every religion there is love.

Yet love has no religion.

"I believe in God, but not as one thing, not as an old man in the sky. I believe that what people call God is something in all of us. I believe that what Jesus and Mohammed and Buddha and the rest said was right. It's just that the translations have gone wrong."

–John Lennon

When you open your Bible, ask the Author to open your heart.

"The meaning of life is to find your gift.

The purpose of life is to give it away."

–Pablo Picasso

Prayer is when you talk to God.

Meditation is when you listen to God.

God can turn broken pieces into masterpieces.

It's not a religion.

It's a relationship.

Always pray to have eyes that see the best in people, a heart that forgives the worst, a mind that forgets the bad, and a soul that never loses faith in God.

Don't be ashamed of your story.

It will inspire others.

Everyone is gifted.

But some people never open their package.

Be the light that helps others see.

Life is a one-time offer.

Use it well.

There is a story they tell of two dogs. Both at separate times walk into the same room. One comes out wagging his tail, while the other comes out growling.

A woman watching this goes into the room to see what could possibly make one dog so happy and the other so mad.

To her surprise, she finds a room filled with mirrors.

The happy dog found a thousand happy dogs looking back at him, while the angry dog saw only angry dogs growling back at him.

What you see in the world around you is a reflection of who you are.

"Maybe you are searching among the branches
for what only appears in the roots."

–Rumi

"Do your little bit of good where you are.

It's those little bits of good put together that overwhelm the world."

-Archbishop Desmond Tutu

Life is better when you are happy but life is best when other people are happy because of you.

Be an inspiration:

Give peace, share your smile.

"Always choosing peace rather than the need to be right reduces tension.

Besides, being right is a matter of perspective.

Being peaceful is simply a choice."

–Karen Casey
All We Have Is All We Need

Don't let your ears witness what your eyes didn't see.

Don't let your mouth speak what your heart doesn't feel.

Live an honest life.

Live without pretending.

Love without depending.

Listen without defending.

Speak without offending.

"There are only two energies at the core of the human experience: love and fear.

Love grants freedom, fear takes it away.

Love invites full expression, fear punishes it.

Love invites you always to break the bonds of ignorance."

–Neale D. Walsch

"Love is the absence of judgment."

–Dalai Lama

"The world is changed by your example, not by your opinion."

–Paulo Coelho

"Blessed are the weird people – poets, misfits, writers, mystics, painters, troubadours – for they teach us to see the world through different eyes."

–Jacob Nordby

We build too many walls and not enough bridges.

"As many colors of the rainbow are an outcome of one pure light, the many religions of the world are an expression of one divine source."

–Sadhguru

"God has given you one face, and you make yourself another."

–William Shakespeare

"Jesus preached this, Mohammed preached this, Buddha preached this. It's in every Holy Book.

'Love thy neighbor as thyself.'

OK?

So you cannot use religion to treat other people badly.

You cannot use God's name to treat other people badly."

–Madonna

Tired of waiting for a miracle to happen?

Then, make your own.

Indian Ten Commandments

The earth is our mother, care for her.

Honor all your relations.

Open your heart and soul to the Great Spirit.

All life is sacred, treat all beings with respect.

Take from the earth what is needed and nothing more.

Do what needs to be done for the good of all.

Give constant thanks to the Great Spirit for every new day.

Speak the truth but only of the good of others.

Follow the rhythms of nature; rise and retire with the sun.

Enjoy life's journey but leave no tracks.

"The music is not in the notes, but in the silence in between."

–Wolfgang Amadeus Mozart

"Kindness is the language which the deaf can hear and the blind can see."

–Mark Twain

Life is an echo.

What you send out - comes back.

What you sow - you reap.

What you give - you get.

What you see in others - exists in you.

Remember: life is an echo.

It always gets back to you.

So, give goodness.

Do you seriously believe God will judge someone for loving a person of the same sex ...

... but will not judge you for hating someone you have never even met?

The Gospel is a declaration, not a debate.

"To speak gratitude is courteous and pleasant. To enact gratitude is generous and noble. But to live gratitude is to touch heaven."

–Johannes A. Gaertner

A man asked Lord Buddha,
"I want happiness."

Lord Buddha said,
"First remove 'I,' that's ego.

Then remove 'Want,' that's desire.

See, now you are left with only 'happiness.'"

"May your soul live in a place of Grace, where Love is Life, and Life is Love."

–Julie Parker

"The best and most beautiful things in the world cannot be seen or even touched ... they must be felt with the heart."

–Helen Keller

There are some people who could hear you speak a thousand words and still not understand you.

And there are others who will understand without you even speaking a word.

"If this is going to be a Christian nation that doesn't help the poor, either we have to pretend that Jesus was just as selfish as we are, or we've got to acknowledge that He commanded us to love the poor and serve the needy without condition and then admit that we just don't want to do it."

–Stephen Colbert

"Jesus, the Alive One, the Loving One, the One who had the courage to be himself under every set of circumstances, was and is the life where God has been seen and can still be seen in a human form under the limitations of our human finitude."

–Bishop John Shelby Spong

"The United States did not create human rights. In a very real sense, it is the other way around: Human rights created the United States."

–Jimmy Carter

"If you cannot find Christ in the beggar at the church door, you will not find Him in the chalice."

–St. John Chrysostom

Maybe it's not always about trying to fix something broken.

Maybe it's about starting over and creating something better.

Nobody is born with hatred and intolerance.

It is ok to doubt what you have been taught to believe.

I asked God to take away my habit.
God said, No.
It is not for me to take away, but for you to give it up.

I asked God to make my handicapped child whole.
God said, No.
His spirit is whole, his body is only temporary.

I asked God to grant me patience.
God said, No.
Patience is a byproduct of tribulations;
it isn't granted, it is learned.

I asked God to give me happiness.
God said, No.
I give you blessings; Happiness is up to you.

I asked God to spare me pain.
God said, No.
Suffering draws you apart from worldly cares
and brings you closer to me.

I asked God to make my spirit grow.
God said, No.
You must grow on your own, but I will prune you
to be fruitful.

I asked God for all things that I might enjoy life.
God said, No.
I will give you life, so that you may enjoy all things.

I asked God to help me love others, as much as God loves me.
God said ...
Ahhhhhhhh, finally you have the idea!

"All things share the same breath: the beast, the tree, the man.

The air shares its spirit with all the life it supports."

–Chief Seattle

"Truly, Allah does not change the conditions of a people until they change what is in themselves."

–Quran 13:11

Ecclesia semper reformanda est …

"The Church is always to be reformed" was a key tenet of the Protestant Reformation. It means that God desires the polity and policy of God's Church to be continually open to appraisal and change.

'God said it, that settles it' is not faithful. It is heretical."

–John Shore

"Holding on to anger is like grasping a hot coal with the intent of throwing it at someone else; you are the one who gets burned."

–Buddha

"No one has ever become poor by giving."

–Anne Frank

May the sun
bring you new energy by day.

May the moon
softly restore you by night.

May the rain
wash away your worries.

May the breeze
blow new strength into your being.

May you walk gently through the world and know
its beauty all the days of your life.

–Apache Blessing

"Be Not Proud
of race, face, place, or grace."

–C.H. Spurgeon

"Being humble means recognizing that we are not on earth to see how important we can become, but to see how much difference we can make in the lives of others."

–Gordon B. Hinckley

"It's impossible," said pride.

"It's risky," said experience.

"It's pointless," said reason.

"Give it a try," whispered the heart.

Christian nation?

So, America was founded on a foreign-born, brown-skinned, Jewish guy who never spoke a word of English, fed and healed the poor for free, defended a woman from being slut-shamed and killed, and chose not to conform to either religious or political nonsense?

Cool!

When are we gonna start this?

"He who begins by loving Christianity better than truth will proceed by loving his own sect or church better than Christianity, and end in loving himself better than all."

–Samuel Taylor Coleridge

"Before you speak to me about your religion, first show it to me in how you treat other people. Before you tell me how much you love your God, show me in how much you love all His children. Before you preach to me of the passion for your faith, teach me about it through your compassion for your neighbors. In the end, I'm not as interested in what you have to tell or sell as in how you choose to live and give."

–Cory Booker, Mayor
Newark, New Jersey

You can never cross the ocean unless you have the courage to lose sight of the shore.

"If people are good only because they fear punishment and hope for reward, then we are a sorry lot indeed."

–Albert Einstein

Everyone smiles in the same language.

"Why extremists always focus on women remains a mystery to me. But they all seem to. It doesn't matter what country they're in or what religion they claim. They all want to control women."

–Hilary Clinton

Forgiveness is not something we do for other people.

We do it for ourselves ... to get well and move on.

"Prayer is not asking. It is a longing of the soul. It is a daily admission of one's weakness.

It is better in prayer to have a heart without words than words without a heart."

–Mahatma Gandhi

"You can safely assume that you've created God in your own image when it turns out that God hates all the same people you do."

–Anne Lamott

"God opens millions of flowers without forcing the buds ... reminding us not to force anything, for things happen perfectly in time."

–Nishan Panwar

"When the government puts its imprimatur on a particular religion, it conveys a message of exclusion to all those who do not adhere to the favored beliefs. A government cannot be premised on the belief that all persons are created equal when it asserts that God prefers some."

–Harry A. Blackmun,
Associate Justice of the Supreme Court of the United States

"Hope is the thing with feathers that perches in the soul and sings the tunes without the words and never stops at all."

–Emily Dickinson

"The best teachers are those who show you where to look, but don't tell you what to see."

–Alexandra K. Trenfor

Jacob was a cheater, Peter had a temper, David had an affair, Noah got drunk, Jonah ran from God, Paul was a murderer, Miriam was a gossip, Martha was a worrier, Gideon was insecure, Thomas was a doubter, Sarah was impatient, Elijah was depressed, Moses stuttered, Zachaeus was short, Abraham was old, and Lazarus was dead.

God doesn't call the qualified; God qualifies the called.

"The grace of God is what sets Christianity apart from every other religion."

–Michael A. Youssef

"If you think you are too small to make a difference, try sleeping with a mosquito."

–Dalai Lama

"God is not a Christian. God is not a Jew or a Muslim or a Hindu or a Buddhist.

I honor my tradition. I walk through my tradition. But I don't believe my tradition defines God.

It only points me to God."

–Bishop John Shelby Spong

The Dalai Lama, when asked what surprised him most about humanity, answered "Man. Because he sacrifices his health to make money. Then he sacrifices money to recuperate his health. And then he is so anxious about the future that he does not enjoy the present; the result being that he does not live in the present or the future; he lives as if he is never going to die, and then dies having never really lived."

I may not have everything I want in life, but I'm blessed enough to have all that I need!

For this, I am grateful.

"Everybody is a genius. But if you judge a fish by its ability to climb a tree, it will live its whole life believing that it is stupid."

–Albert Einstein

"The church is a hospital for sinners, not a museum for saints."

–Abigail Van Buren

"Religion is for people who are afraid of going to hell.

Spirituality is for those who have already been there."

–Vine Deloria, Sioux

If you spend time condemning others instead of loving your neighbor, you're doing it wrong.

There are people who always seem to be looking for conflicts.

If you meet them, walk away.

The battle they are fighting isn't with you, it is within themselves.

"The purpose of religion is to control yourself, not to criticize others. How much am I doing about my anger, attachment, hatred, pride and jealousy? These are the things which we must check in our daily lives."

–Dalai Lama

"Love is the greatest gift we can give or receive."

–Anthony Douglas Williams
Inside the Divine Pattern

Other cultures are not failed attempts at being you.

The most valuable places in the world to be are in someone's thoughts, someone's prayers, and someone's heart.

"We must all mature in our faith to the point where we can separate our faith in God from the human and fallible church. We must develop our personal life of prayer so that we have our own direct and immediate contact with God. We can no longer allow our faith and belief to depend exclusively on the mediation of the church, with the result that if we become disillusioned with and scandalized by the human church, we are tempted to give up all belief. We must take a chance on God, keeping in mind that God, too, may well be scandalized by the church. After all, during his lifetime Jesus was in serious conflict with his church and its authorities."

–John J. McNeill,
Taking A Chance On God

"Hospitality is politically subversive."

–Richard Beck

"We're not in this struggle because we're following a particular agenda. It's precisely because we believe in the kind of God depicted in the Scriptures and in the life of our Lord and Savior Jesus Christ. It is quite exhilarating to speak about a God who has an incredible bias, a notorious bias in favor of the downtrodden. You look at Exodus and the Israelites' escape from a bottomless pit. God is not evenhanded. God is biased up to his eyebrows."

–Archbishop Desmond Tutu

"An intelligent person will open your mind, a beautiful person will open your eyes and a loving, kind person will open your heart."

–Lana Marconi, Ph.D.

Hope is putting faith to work when doubting would be easier.

"There is always something to do. There are hungry people to feed, naked people to clothe, sick people to comfort and make well. And while I don't expect you to save the world I do think it's not asking too much for you to love those with whom you sleep, share the happiness of those whom you call friend, engage those among you who are visionary and remove from your life those who offer you depression, despair and disrespect."

-Nikki Giovanni

No one is born with hatred or intolerance.

"We do not entirely understand what 'resurrection' means, but if we have understood the story, we should be 'holding fast' to what we do know: that Jesus goes before us, summoning us to the way of the cross. And that is the hardest ending of all: not tragedy, not victory, but an unending challenge to follow anew. Because that means we must respond."

–Ched Myers,
Binding The Strong Man

"I am not the only one who sees the underside and God at the same time. There are lots of us, and we are at home in the biblical stories of antiheroes and people who don't get it; beloved prostitutes and rough fishermen ...

It was here in the midst of my own community of underside dwellers that I couldn't help but begin to understand the Gospel, the life-changing reality that God is not far off, but here among the brokenness of our lives. And having seen it, I couldn't help but point it out."

–Nadia Bolz-Weber,
Pastrix

"Our role is not to defend certain propositions about Christ, but to affirm the person of Christ, by assisting one another to discern the presence of Christ in our lives, and then developing the capacity to process our lives - our cultures, our traditions, and our religions - in relation to the Spirit of Christ."

–Dave Andrews,
Christi-Anarchy

Evolution means that God is not finished with us yet.

"I do not ask to see the reason for it all; I ask only to share the wonder of it all."

–Brennan Manning,
The Ragamuffin Gospel

"Some people believe the alternative to bad religion is secularism, but that is wrong ...

The answer to bad religion is better religion: prophetic rather than partisan, broad and deep instead of narrow, and based on values as opposed to ideology."

–Jim Wallis

Be yourself no matter what other people think.

God made you the way you are for a reason.

Besides, an original is always worth more than a copy!

May the sun bring you new energy by day.

May the moon softly restore you by night.

May the rain wash away your worries.

May the breeze blow new strength into your being.

May you walk gently through the world and know its beauty all the days of your life.

–Apache Blessing

At the end of life, what really matters is not what we bought but what we built; not our competence but our character; and not our success but our significance.

Live a life that matters.

Live a life of love.

"Believe in your dreams. They were given to you for a reason."

–Katrina Mayer

Be nice to someone you don't really like.

Change the world ... one enemy at a time.

When you come to the edge of all light that you know and are about to drop off into the darkness of the unknown, faith is knowing that one of two things will happen:

There will be something solid to stand on or you will be taught to fly.

"How ironic is it that hardly any major religion has looked at science and concluded, 'This is better than we thought! The Universe is much bigger than our prophets said, grander, more subtle, more elegant!'

Instead they say, 'No, no, no! My god is a little god, and I want him to stay that way.'

A religion, old or new, that stressed the magnificence of the Universe as revealed by modern science might be able to draw forth reserves of reverence and awe hardly tapped by the conventional faiths."

–Carl Sagan

"Change will not come if we wait for some other person or some other time. We are the ones we've been waiting for. We are the change that we seek."

–Barack Obama

Character is how you treat those who can do nothing for you.

Oh, Great Spirit who made all races:

Look kindly upon the whole human family and take away the arrogance and hatred which separates us from our brothers.

–Cherokee Prayer

"When we needed the outer form of a savior, You were there for us.

When our conscious mind matures, we turn within rather than without to find You there, not separate or apart but one in the same with ourselves.

We are moving toward Christ consciousness."

–Maureen Ramsey Hughes

" ... solitude begins with a time and a place for God, and God alone.

If we really believe not only that God exists but also that God is actively present in our lives – healing, teaching and guiding – we need to set aside a time and space to give God our undivided attention."

–Henri J.M. Nouwen

"The world is a dangerous place, not because of those who do evil ... but because of those who look on and do nothing."

–Albert Einstein

"Sometimes, when I hear people talking about God, I feel like an atheist.

The God they speak of, I don't believe in:

A God who loves Christians but hates Muslims; or a God who pours luxuries on the rich but consigns the poor to poverty, or a God who cares about human souls but doesn't care about preserving and protecting our beautiful planet.

So if you ask me, 'Is God real?' I first have to ask, 'Which God are we talking about? And what do you mean by God?'"

–Brian McLaren

"Believing that your faith tradition alone contains God is like believing the rain falls only in your cup."

–John Shore

A society grows great when old men plant trees whose shade they know they shall never sit in.

–Greek Proverb

"A boat is safe in the harbor. But this is not the purpose of the boat."

–Paulo Coelho

An arrow can only be shot by pulling it backward.

When life is dragging you back with difficulties, just imagine that it's going to launch you into something great!

Your beliefs don't make you a better person, your behavior does.

To those I may have wronged, I ask forgiveness.

To those I may have helped, I wish I did more.

To those I neglected to help, I ask for understanding.

To those who have helped me, I sincerely thank you so much.

Have a renewing, meaningful, holy week!

"You are the universe expressing itself as a human for a little while."

–Eckhart Tolle

"If it's hard for us to accept our monsters and love them and free them to become the beautiful creatures they were meant to be, it's even harder for most of us to believe in the happy ending."

–Madeleine L'Engle,
The Rock That Is Higher

Don't be trapped by DOGMA ...

which is living with the results of other people's thinking.

"What is intriguing about this story is the sequence. Jesus touches the leper first. Then the command 'Be clean!' is offered. That is, Jesus' first move is into ritual defilement. By first touching the leper, Jesus intentionally and willfully seeks contamination, standing in solidarity with the unclean. This is striking because the expected sequence would be the initial purification followed by contact. Jesus, surprisingly for the onlookers, does the opposite. Contact occurs first. Purification follows solidarity. And one can only wonder how various Christian communities approach this sequence in their own missional endeavors."

–Richard Beck,
Unclean

" ... in the circle of life, we are all connected."

–Mufasa teaching Simba,
The Lion King

Life doesn't always introduce you to the people you want to meet. Sometimes, life puts you in touch with the people you need to meet: to help you, to hurt you, to leave you, to love you, and to gradually strengthen you into the person you were meant to become.

It's easier to build up a child than it is to repair an adult.

Choose your words wisely.

"I do not judge people by the scriptures of their faith or the scars from their past.

I embrace them by the content of their hearts."

–Dodinksy

Now that we're done talking about the end of the world, maybe we can focus on making this the beginning of a better one.

"And while I stood there I saw more than I can tell and I understood more than I saw: for I was seeing in a sacred manner the shapes of all things in the spirit, and the shape of all shapes as they must live together like one being."

–Black Elk
Wichasha Wakan Oglala Lakota

Why do we close our eyes when we pray, cry, kiss, dream?

Because the most beautiful things in life are not seen but felt only by the heart.

"Cowardice asks the question, 'Is it safe?'

Expediency asks the question, 'Is it politic?'

But conscience asks the question, 'Is it right?'

And there comes a time when one must take a position that is neither safe, nor politic, nor popular but because conscience tells one it is right."

–Martin Luther King, Jr., Jr.

Create a life that feels on the inside, not one that just looks good on the outside.

Dear God,

I don't ask you to make my life easier, but I ask you to give me the strength to face all my troubles.

According to the Bible, all of mankind descended from one man and one woman ... who had two sons.

Think about that.

Take all the time that you need.

"I can't for the life of me imagine that God will say, 'I will punish you because you are black, you should have been white; I will punish you because you are a woman, you should have been a man; I will punish you because you are homosexual, you ought to have been heterosexual.' I can't for the life of me believe that is how God sees things."

–Archbishop Desmond Tutu

A truly happy person is one who can enjoy the scenery while on a detour.

"The idea that some lives matter less is the root of all that is wrong with the world."

–Dr. Paul Farmer

"Be not forgetful to entertain strangers, for thereby some have entertained angels unawares."

–Hebrews 13:2

Envy:

Blowing out the other person's candle will not make yours shine brighter.

Forgive others not because they deserve forgiveness, but because you deserve peace.

To forgive is to set a prisoner free ...

... and realizing that prisoner is you.

Anyone can hold a grudge, but it takes a person with character to forgive.

When you forgive, you release yourself from a painful burden.

Forgiveness doesn't mean what happened was OK, and it doesn't mean that person should still be welcome in your life.

It just means you have made peace with the pain, and are ready to let it go.

"If a man is to survive, he will have learned to take a delight in the essential differences between men and between cultures. He will learn that differences in ideas and attitudes are a delight, part of life's exciting variety, not something to fear."

–Gene Roddenberry

"You give but little when you give of your possessions. It is when you give of yourself that you truly give."

–Kahill Gibran

"The feeling remains that God is on the journey, too."

−Saint Teresa of Avila

The greatest test of faith is when you don't get what you want, but still you are able to say, "Thank you, Lord."

"It is wonderful how much time good people spend fighting the devil.

If they would only expend the same amount of energy loving their fellow men, the devil would die in his own tracks of ennui."

–Helen Keller

"Before you act, listen.

Before you react, think.

Before you spend, earn.

Before you criticize, wait.

Before you pray, forgive.

Before you quit, try."

–Ernest Hemingway

After all of this is over, all that will really matter
is how we treated each other.

O God, you are the God of peace and I am a worrier.

Take away my worry and give me some of your peace.

Help me not to waste my time worrying about things about which there is nothing to be done, but help me to accept them, and to overcome them.

Lord, grant me a quiet night and peaceful sleep.

Amen.

"If we have no peace, it is because we have forgotten that we belong to each other."

–Mother Teresa

I've seen and met angels wearing the disguise of ordinary people, living ordinary lives.

"I am not an advocate for frequent changes in laws and constitutions. But laws and institutions must go hand in hand with the progress of the human mind. As that becomes more developed, more enlightened, as new discoveries are made, new truths discovered and manners and opinions change with this change of circumstances, institutions must advance also to keep pace with the times. We might as well require a man to wear still the coat which fitted him when a boy as civilized society to remain ever under the regimen of their barbarous ancestors."

–Thomas Jefferson

"There are four questions of value in life:

What is sacred?

Of what is the spirit made?

What is worth living for?

And what is worth dying for?

The answer to each is the same:

Only love."

–Johnny Depp

"This is my simple religion. There is no need for temples; no need for complicated philosophy.

Our own brain, our own heart is our temple: the philosophy is kindness."

–Dalai Lama

"Sometimes your only available transportation is a leap of faith."

–Margaret Shepard

"Being a Christian is less about cautiously avoiding sin than about courageously and actively doing God's will."

–Dietrich Bonhoeffer

Life is a balance of holding on and letting go.

Life isn't about waiting for the storm to pass …

It's about learning to dance in the rain.

"Love and compassion are necessities, not luxuries.

Without them, humanity cannot survive."

–Dalai Lama

Learn to love with all your heart and accept the unlovable side of others.

For anyone can love a rose, but only a great heart can include the thorns.

Love your parents.

We are so busy growing up, we often forget they are also growing old.

"We make a living by what we get.
But we make a life by what we give."

–Winston Churchill

"Never, never be afraid to do what's right, especially if the well-being of a person or animal is at stake. Society's punishments are small compared to the wounds we inflict on our soul when we look the other way."

–Martin Luther King, Jr.

Don't judge my path if you haven't walked my journey.

Never look down on someone ...

Unless you are helping them get up!

"New beginnings are often disguised as painful endings."

–Lao Tzu

"People take different roads seeking fulfillment and happiness.

Just because they're not on your road doesn't mean they've gotten lost."

–H. Jackson Brown

"Whenever anyone has offended me, I try to raise my soul so high that the offense cannot reach it."

–Rene Descartes

"Peace begins with a smile."

–Mother Teresa

People were created to be loved.

Things were created to be used.

The reason why the world is in chaos is because things are being loved and people are being used.

Pray hardest when it is hardest to pray.

"Relative to other religions, the Christian's choice is clear: to believe that either everyone who is not a Christian has tragically failed, or that God is so great, vast, and unimaginatively creative that, for reasons no one can begin to fathom, He/She chose to manifest in different ways to different peoples at different times. One might call it the choice between sheer ego and common sense."

–John Shore

Religions are perspectives, not truths.

But this does not make them untrue.

People who want to share their religious views with you almost never want you to share yours with them.

"The essence of true religious teaching is that one should serve and befriend all."

–M. K. Gandhi

Man says, "Show me and I'll trust you."

God says, "Trust me and I'll show you."

"There is no such thing as a simple act of compassion or an inconsequential act of service.

Everything we do for another person has infinite consequences."

–Caroline Myss

You are strong when you know your weaknesses.

You are beautiful when you appreciate your flaws.

You are wise when you learn from your mistakes.

"I distrust those people who know so well what God wants them to do, because I notice it always coincides with their own desires."

–Susan B. Anthony

When you are going through difficulty and wonder where God is, remember that the teacher is always quiet during the test.

The real reason why we can't have the Ten Commandments in a courthouse:

You cannot post "Thou shalt not steal," "Thou shalt not commit adultery," and "Thou shalt not lie" in a building full of lawyers, judges, and politicians.

It creates a hostile work environment.

The church should be about multiplication, not division.

–Acts 2:47

"Our lives begin to end the day we become silent about things that matter."

–Martin Luther King, Jr.

The moment you're ready to quit is usually the moment right before a miracle happens.

Don't give up.

"The sole meaning of life is to serve humanity."

–Leo Tolstoy

Sometimes the strongest people are the ones who love beyond all faults, cry behind closed doors, and fight battles that nobody knows about.

"When we look at another human being and fail to see a beloved sister or brother, there will always be a 'them' and an 'us.'"

–Heather McCloskey Beck

Three wise women

Would have asked for directions,

Arrived on time,

Helped deliver the baby,

Brought practical gifts,

Cleaned the stable,

Made a casserole,

And there would be Peace on Earth!

Time & Karma

When a bird is alive, it eats ants.
When the bird dies, ants eat it.

One tree can be made into a million matchsticks. But only one matchstick is needed to burn a million trees.

Circumstances can change at any time.

Don't devalue or hurt anyone in this life.

You may be powerful today, but time is more powerful than you!

Trusting God means we believe when we cannot see.

–Hebrews 11:1-3

An old Cherokee told his grandson, "My son, there is a battle between two wolves inside us all.

One is Evil. It is anger, jealousy, greed, resentment, inferiority, lies and ego.

The other is Good. It is joy, peace, love, hope, humility, kindness, empathy, and truth.

The boy thought about it and asked, "Grandfather, which wolf wins?"

The old man quietly replied, "The one you feed."

"Modern man suffers from a kind of poverty of the spirit, which stands in glaring contrast with a scientific and technological abundance.

We've learned to fly the air as birds, we've learned to swim the seas as fish, yet we haven't learned to walk the Earth as brothers and sisters."

–Martin Luther King, Jr.

Resurrection is the hope that those wounds, those dead parts of ourselves, can be overcome.

It is a hope that all things can and will be made right, no matter how long it takes.

Whoever has lived or died before us has no bearing on that hope.

We choose to stand at the tomb and wait expectantly for the world to begin again.

We are the resurrection.

Wisdom is knowing the right path to take.

Integrity is taking it.

"I cannot do all the good the world needs, but the world needs all the good that I can do."

–Jana Stanfield

"The tragedy of life is not death, but what we let die inside of us while we live."

–Norman Cousins

"The test of our progress is not whether we add more to the abundance of those who have much; it is whether we provide enough for those who have little."

–Franklin D. Roosevelt

"Many on the 'Christian Right' are fond of posing the question 'WWJD?—What would Jesus do?'

I'd like to remind them what Jesus DID do:

He cared for the poor. He did not condemn the woman caught in adultery. He prayed alone. He commanded us to love our enemies. He preached peace. He ate, drank, and lived with 'tax collectors and sinners' – the lowlifes and outcasts of his day – while reserving his condemnation for the religious leaders who from a place of privilege imposed their legalism and literalism on the people they were responsible for leading. He told his disciples not to oppose the healing work of those outside the ranks of his followers. And again and again he reminded us to care for the poor.

Whatever Jesus would do, given what he did do, and has promised he will do, I don't think it looks much like what the insulated, self-congratulatory … fans on the 'Christian Right' are doing."

–Marilyn Chandler McEntyre, Ph.D.

"You must learn a new way to think before you can master a new way to be."

–Marianne Williamson

www.ingramcontent.com/pod-product-compliance
Lightning Source LLC
Chambersburg PA
CBHW071646090426
42738CB00009B/1440